THE ALL-COLOUR VEGETARIAN RECIPE BOOK

W. Foulsham & Company Limited
Yeovil Road, Slough, Berkshire, SL1 4JH

ISBN 0-572-01403-1

Originally published by Falken-Verlag GmbH, Niedernhausen/TS West Germany.
Photographs copyright © 1985 Falken-Verlag
This English language edition copyright © 1987 W. Foulsham & Co. Ltd.
Printed in Hong Kong.

THE ALL-COLOUR VEGETARIAN RECIPE BOOK

Edited by Christopher & Jean Conil

W. Foulsham & Co. Ltd.
London • New York • Toronto •
Cape Town • Sydney

Foreword

Before reading this book, or setting off to the kitchen to begin cooking, there are a few general instructions which apply to all of the recipes.

Unless otherwise specified, each dish will serve 4 — 6 people.

Although there are three sets of measurements included with each recipe, you should choose one set only and follow it rigidly when cooking. For precision it is best to use the metric measurements. Volumetric measurements are recommended only if you have standard cups and spoons.

Where yeast is used in a recipe we have given instructions for reconstituting dried yeast. You can of course use fresh yeast or dried yeast that does not need to be reconstituted, but the recipes should then be altered accordingly.

Crème fraîche is frequently specified in recipes. It is similar to single (light cream), but contains more acid. If crème fraîche is not available, add the juice of ¼ lemon to each 100g/4oz of single cream. You can also substitute soured cream.

Wherever herbs are used, the quantity given is for fresh herbs. If you are using dried herbs, use half the quantity only.

Unless otherwise specified, tomatoes should always be peeled and seeded. To do this, make a slit in the skin and plunge the tomato in boiling salted water for 30 seconds. Peel the skin, cut the tomato in half horizontally and squeeze gently to remove the seeds.

Contents

Introduction

For many years now Christopher and I have been involved in the production of vegetarian cookery books and diets. Through our work in the creative formulation of recipes in association with the many food processing companies which specialize in health products, we have become very aware of what is needed to give natural diet menus the best ingredients not only from the health point of view but also in terms of taste and presentation. The pleasure of eating cannot be ignored, no matter how nutritious the food.

Following the enormous success of Jean Conil's *Cuisine Vegetarienne Française*, with its typical Gallic traditions, we were more than delighted to be asked to edit this new book from Europe which we consider to be one of the best vegetarian cookery books available anywhere in the world. All cooks — whether vegetarian or non-vegetarian — should include this title in their kitchen library. It is a worthy companion to our own *Cuisine Vegetarienne Française*, and will more than complement it as a work of art in the field of natural eating.

Following precise and highly informative sections on the need for the correct diet and the range of nutrients available, the book opens with a selection of suggested menus for all occasions. These are especially well balanced. In the recipe sections, there are many starters with 'modern' flavours. Many of the soups can almost be considered as meals in their own right, such is their high nutritional value. One particular delight is the use of kohlrabi, an unusual turnip-like vegetable rarely featured in British menus yet quite widely available in supermarkets.

The chapter on rice and grains contains many interesting recipes, ranging from Italian risottos to light roulades. Others, such as casserole of rye with asparagus, will also prove to be a delight. Barley, oats, buckwheat and millet are among the cereals used in their original, natural way, and there are also many new variations for pasta, ravioli and lasagne. You may love Boursin cheese, but try quark; it tastes better still!

The main dishes contain a collection of favourites as well as new recipes to make your meals a treat without having to consider meat, fish or poultry. They unreservedly prove the theory that vegetarian food can encourage converts on the strength of its taste alone! Vegetables have been used in a variety of interesting and imaginative ways to ensure that there are dishes to please everyone. The salads likewise make good use of a huge range of fresh fruits and vegetables, and the chapter is well supplied with ideas for producing mouthwatering masterpieces of freshness and quality.

The desserts and baked surprises offer a selection to tempt young and old, including those with a sweet tooth as well as those who prefer dishes with less sweetness. Semolina slices with raspberry sauce, waffles with cressy quark, fruit pizza, yoghurt torte and a rich selection of muesli — all combine to make this course as memorable as all the others.

The All-Colour Vegetarian Recipe Book wins the Gold Medal, as far as we are concerned, for its originality, richness of ideas, and very simple yet excellent recipes.

The Editors
Master Chef Jean Conil.
President of the Society of Master Chefs.
Master Baker Christopher Conil.
1987

7

Why Do We Need Food?

We could simply say: in order to live. But there is more to it. Biologically, life consists of the synthesis, disintegration and modification of living substances. Food is broken down in the body by a series of physical and chemical processes to release energy. The energy is then used to repair cells, build new cells and to provide movement. This process is called metabolism and to keep it going, we need a constant supply of energy in the form of food.

The Right Diet

Today, we have all come to realize the importance of correct nutrition for maintaining our health. Therefore it can only be considered irresponsible for people with access to the proper foods to regard eating and drinking as matters of mere necessity or mere pleasure. Good health and a long life, which we all aim for, are influenced to a great extent by our food intake.

Nutrients

We distinguish between nutrients which yield energy (proteins, fats and carbohydrates) and those which yield no energy (vitamins, minerals, fibre and water). The amount of nutrients required by an individual depends on many factors — environmental influences, age, race, body build, work and leisure activities, to name just a few. Some nutrients are described as vital; in other words they are absolutely necessary for the human body. These substances must be given to the body regularly in the form of food, since unbalanced nutrition deprives the body of important 'building bricks', resulting in deficiency diseases. We should try, therefore, to make our weekly menu as varied as possible, but at the same time restricting our total intake as much of the surplus food we eat is stored as fat, and is detrimental to our health.

Protein

Protein is a vital nutrient which the body must have in correct quantities. Its function is to build up and maintain the muscles and inner organs. Without protein, a child's body will not grow, nor will its cells be renewed. It is also important to consume the right type of protein to ensure a sufficient intake of the eight essential amino acids.

The amount of protein required differs from person to person according to age, build and the type of work done. An adult should take in about 0.8g (0.03 oz) of protein per kg (2.2 lb) of body weight. Not every sort of protein is of equal value, however; this variation is called the biological balance of protein. The more similar the food protein is to body protein, the more valuable it is, as the body needs to consume less to achieve the required amount.

The calorific value of 1g (0.04 oz) protein amounts to 4.1 kcal (kilocalories) or 17kJ (kilojoule). Only ovo-lacto vegetarians and lacto-vegetarians can achieve their required intake of protein with eggs, milk and dairy products. Strict vegetarians must supply their bodies with protein through combinations of diverse foods — for instance, the soya bean as all soya bean products yield biologically valuable protein. Vegans of course do not eat eggs or dairy animal products, making it vital for them to find alternative sources of protein.

Fat

Fat plays an important role in nutrition, although the steep increase in the number of overweight people in the Western World is partly due to over-consumption of fat.

Fat should not simply be condemned, however, because it is also an important nutrient and contains the fat-soluble vitamins A and E. So some fat must be included in the diet, but it should be incorporated into our menus with care: 1g (0.04 oz) fat yields 9.3 kcal or 38kJ.

Generally, fats are described as being animal or vegetable or, according to their consistency, as hard, soft or liquid. The melting point of a certain kind of fat influences its digestibility; the closer the melting point is to the body temperature, the easier the fat is to digest. All fats are composed of glycerine and various fatty acids which are again divided into saturated, unsaturated and polyunsaturated. Saturated, or animal fats, contain cholesterol which is needed for building up hormones and gall liquid. Too much cholesterol in the blood can lead to arteriosclerosis and heart disease and should therefore be kept to a minimum, so we are now advised to use unsaturated, or vegetable fats, rather than saturated fats. Linseed, sunflower, soya and corn oil are particularly recommended.

Carbohydrates

Carbohydrates consist of carbon, hydrogen and oxygen and are vital for providing energy: 1g (0.04 oz) carbohydrates yields 4.1kcal or 17kJ.

Carbohydrates can be divided into primary sugar (glucose, fructose, etc.), sucrose (from cane and beet), lactose (from milk) and maltose (from starch, cellulose and pectin).

Starch is of special importance in our diet. Carbohydrates occur in rice, cereals, corn, potatoes and other roots such as yams, fruit and vegetables. Refined crystallized sugar is a 'no-go' in terms of conscious good nutrition — it is responsible among other things for caries and obesity in many people. The body transforms unused carbohydrates into fat and stores it in fat deposits within the body.

Minerals

Minerals are inorganic substances, some of which are vital for the human body. These essential minerals are needed for the metabolism, but they also influence the functioning of the nerves. Apart from that they fulfil special tasks such as building the bones, parts of the teeth, hormones and enzymes. A well-balanced diet will provide sufficient minerals.

Some minerals appear in greater amounts in our bodies, for instance potash, sodium, magnesium, phosphorus, calcium, chloride, and sulphur. Others appear only in minute traces within our bodies; the most important of these are iodine, iron, cobalt, copper, manganese and zinc. Their main task is to catalyze enzymes into action, transport nutrients and build up blood and hormones.

Even today, we are uncertain about the importance of many minerals. Some of them are even toxic in large quantities.

Vitamins

Vitamins are vital for human beings. As the body is incapable of building up these substances itself from other foodstuffs, they must be taken in with food. Vitamins provide no energy, but they are essential for directing and regulating the metabolism. If the intake of vitamins is too low, deficiency diseases will appear. We distinguish between water soluble vitamins (B and C) and fat soluble vitamins (A, D, E and K).

The vitamin content of food can be influenced by the way the dishes are prepared.

In uncooked, untreated food it is highest; therefore fruit and vegetables should be eaten raw or cooked very quickly in only a little water. With cereal dishes, the whole grains with bran should be used wherever possible. Milk and dairy products are important for providing us with vitamins, but try to avoid tinned and ready-made products. Low-fat milk and yoghurt or buttermilk whey are highly recommended.

Fibre

Fibre is the cellulose or plant fibre which we cannot digest and must, therefore, excrete. Fibre swells in the intestines and provides the food base for intestinal micro-organisms, making it vital for healthy, regular digestion. It is found in all kinds of corn, vegetables, salad stuff, fruit and potatoes, but also in wheatgerm and linseed. Our new healthy eating habits have changed drastically in recent years with the Nouvelle Cuisine both accepting and promoting the use of raw vegetables and fruit either as a garnish or complimentary food item. Eating more raw vegetables is recommended for many ailments and eases the process of digestion, hence improving our health generally.

Water

The human body consists of 60–70 percent of water. Because the body loses water constantly it must be replaced in sufficient amounts. One can survive for a longer period of time without food, but without water, the whole metabolism soon comes to a halt.

Water transports substances in our body, but it also serves as a medium for bathing the body organs and keeps the body temperature even. The amount of water a body needs depends on many factors — 35g (1.2 oz) per kg (2.2 lb) of body weight is a guideline. This means 2–2.5 litres/3½–4½ pints daily for the average adult. When drinking water, distilled, spring or mineral water are preferable.

Points to Remember When Shopping

In our modern world, shopping has become relatively easy. Health-food shops, supermarkets or delicatessens are within easy reach of most of us, and these have everything required for vegetarian cooking. You will probably be surprised at the diversity and high quality of the foods on display there. For your information, we have listed the most important products, and a few useful hints. One further tip is to shop frequently for fresh foods. Wilted vegetables, for example, have lost much of their food value.

Drinking-Whey

Drinking-whey is an excellent drink which is also extremely healthy. It consists of milk liquid, minerals, water-soluble milk vitamins, lactic sugar and lactic acid. Drinking-whey is available in various different flavours, either as natural whey or with added fruit. It tastes best when cool. Whey powder can also be used to make a delicious, healthy drink as can buttermilk either as it is or diluted with soda water.

Biogarde

This yoghurt is made from special cultures of milk bacteria in which there is a large quantity of right turning lactic acid which is especially easy for the human body to digest. Quark, quark products and cottage cheese are made in a similar way and are all widely available in shops or simple to make at home. Natural quark is a curd cheese made by the coagulation or curdling of milk casein by lemon juice or a similar acidic agent. Lemon juice produces a soft curd, while vinegar produces a harder, coarser curd.

Milk and Dairy Products

For lacto-vegetarians it is very important to eat the right dairy products. Of course, it's best if you can get milk from a local farmer who rears his cows on organic foodstuffs. Otherwise, you must look for dairy products from organically reared animals, especially goats, in health food shops in order to ensure that the products are free from chemical additives.

Wholewheat Flour

Try to replace white flour and products made from white flour with wholewheat flour as often as possible, as it provides important vitamins and fibre. Be sure that all the wholewheat you buy is grown organically and that it is freshly ground. For fancy pastries, use very finely ground flour. The bran left over after sieving can be used in other dishes, for instance stuffing or soups. Freshly ground flour should be used relatively quickly, since it soon goes rancid and loses all its nutrients.

Soya Products

Apart from soya beans, health-food shops offer a wide variety of soya products. Soya provides high-quality protein and is better than meat or animal protein. With a little imagination, you can make dishes from soya that are very similar to meat dishes and which may influence even the most dedicated opponents of vegetarianism. There are also plenty of ready-made products like goulash, rissoles and spreads which likewise are very tasty.

Tofu is the best soya product. This is soya cheese which is made from ripe, soaked, then cooked soya beans to which are added gelling agents. This mixture is pressed into convenient shapes, without added preservatives, and then packed. In eastern Asia, Tofu has been one of the most important protein sources for more than 2000 years. (See *The Secret of Tofu* by Christopher and Jean Conil, Foulsham.)

Tofu has a more or less bland taste, will accept any flavouring and, due to its texture, can be grilled, baked, fried, steamed or stir-fried Chinese style.

Soya milk is healthier than cow's milk and can replace it in cooking. Soya sauce is produced by fermentation and is used as a flavouring in much modern cookery. Worcester sauce is produced from soya sauce.

Soya flour is the dehydrated form of soya bean. It can replace eggs in many recipes and enrich starchy products with additional protein nutrients.

Oils and Fat

When using oil you should buy only oils made from one fruit, i.e. olive oil, sunflower, soya, peanut or walnut oil, etc. There are several ways of producing oil, but you should choose oil from cold pressings. It is somewhat more expensive but tastes better and is very high in nutrients. This oil is made from fresh, ripe fruit.

Although the choice of butter or vegetable margarine is individual, vegetable margarine contains unsaturated fats and are therefore lower in cholesterol. It is best used in purées, cakes or puddings. For roasting or grilling, food can be lightly brushed with vegetable oil. Deep-fried foods should be avoided wherever possible.

Vinegar

Not all vinegars are the same. In Britain, people prefer malt vinegar, whereas Mediterranean countries tend to use wine vinegar. The Americans prefer cider vinegar because malic acid is less corrosive than the acetic acid in other vinegars. Which kind of vinegar you decide on is a matter of taste, but we would recommend cider vinegar, since it is more wholesome. It is the acidity content which distinguishes the various kinds of vinegar, therefore try a particular type before using it in salads, etc. to ensure the taste is not too acidic for you. The acidity is generally stated on the label

— normal vinegar contains 5 per cent vinegar acid.

You can also enhance your vinegar by adding fruit or herbs. For 1 litre (1.8 pints) of vinegar you will need about 200–300g (7–11 oz) of fruit or 50–100g (2–4 oz) herbs. Transfer the vinegar and herbs to a jar, close the lid well and leave to 'set' for a fortnight, shaking the jar occasionally. Then strain and transfer to a clean bottle ready for use.

Sugar

Sugar should be avoided as much as possible as it makes fat deposits in the body if it is not utilised as energy and can also cause damage to the teeth. Honey consists of glucose, a sweetener which is absorbed into the bloodstream more quickly than sucrose and is therefore a good alternative to other sugars. In Britain, Sweetex liquid or crystals is a great help in reducing sugar intake.

Seasoning Agents

Extracts from vegetable stock or yeast stock are very good for adding flavour, as are spice mixtures and herb salts. Try several — you are sure to find something to your liking. Fresh herbs and spices are best of all.

Brewer's Yeast

Brewer's yeast can provide B vitamins, minerals and protein and serves as an excellent seasoning agent. Brewer's yeast is available as powder, tablets or in a paste form like Marmite or soya paste (miso).

Salt

Salt is one of our basic spices, and a vital part of healthy nutrition. However, too much salt is unhealthy. Salt is divided into cooking salt, table salt, sea salt and various herb salts. Salt is a welcome addition to many dishes, but should be used very sparingly. For vegetarian cooking one should use sea salt or potassium chloride.

Dinner Parties for Every Occasion

Birthday Dinner

Medley of Vegetable Fritters
Wild Herb Soup
Tofu Ragout
Chocolate Cherry Slice

Beer Dinner

Herbed Vegetable Rice
Beetroot and Tofu Soup
Boiled Potatoes with Dips
Semolina Slices with
Raspberry Sauce

Wine Dinner

Celeriac Salad
Mushroom Crescents
Asparagus in White Wine
Sauce
Mixed Fruit Salad with Nuts

Hearty Dinner

Betroot and Tangerine Salad
Sweet and Sour Spinach
Ravioli
Brittany Soup
Italian Cheese Pickle and
Herbed Oat Bread

Italian Dinner

Ratatouille Pie with Cheese
Sauce
Tomato Angelo
Lasagne al Forno
Apricot Tart with Coconut

Chinese Dinner

Peking Soup
Baked Honey Beans
Savoury Choux Fritters
Home-made Almond Ice
Cream

Gourmet Dinner

Tomato Angelo
Spring Vegetable Soup
Quiche Lorraine
Apricot Tart with Coconut

Quick Dinner

Carrot and Orange Salad
Vegetableburgers
Madrid Salad
Rolled Oats with Cherry
Cream

Sunday Dinner

Love Apple Soup
Hungarian Soya Goulash
Baked Potatoes in Soured
Cream Gratin
Fruit Pizza

Light Dinner

Baked Apple Stuffed with
Walnuts
Chinese Egg and Mushroom
Soup
Celeriac Salad
Tutti-Frutti Jelly

Diet Dinner

Tropical Fruit Cocktail
Delicious Carrot Soup
Cabbage and Rice Roulade
Apple Sorbet with Mint

Starters

In vegetarian cuisine particularly, you shouldn't miss out on delicious and light starters — it is mainly vegetable dishes that contain plenty of vitamins and minerals. Starters whet your appetite and prepare you for further delights.

Italian Cheese Pickle

Ingredients	Metric/Imperial
Olive oil	225ml/8fl oz
Chillies, seeded and sliced	2/2
Garlic cloves, chopped	2–4/2–4
Black peppercorns	15ml/1 tbsp
Juniper berries	4/4
Bay leaf	1/1
Rosemary or basil	1sprig/1sprig
Thyme	1 sprig/1 sprig
Spanish onion	1 medium/1 medium
Provolone cheese	100g/4oz
Bel Paese cheese	100g/4oz
Gorgonzola cheese	100g/4oz
Mozzarella cheese	100g/4oz

Slice the onion, cut the cheese into bite-size pieces without any loose crumbs and arrange in a jar. Add the chillies, garlic, herbs and spices.

Pour the oil on top and leave to marinate in the fridge for at least 12 hours.

Drain the cheese and serve with Herbed Oat Bread.

Herbed Oat Bread

Ingredients	Metric/Imperial
Rolled oats	100 g/4 oz
Buttermilk	150–200 ml/5–7 fl oz
Wholewheat flour	250g/9oz
Dried yeast	10g/1 tsp
Butter	30ml/2 tbsp
Sea salt	a pinch/a pinch
Chives, snipped	15ml/1 tbsp
Parsley, chopped	15ml/1 tbsp
Marjoram, chopped	15ml/1 tbsp
Caraway seeds	5ml/1 tsp

Additionally:

Egg yolks, beaten	2/2
Aniseed	15ml/1 tbsp
Cardamom pods	5ml/1 tsp
Caraway seeds	5ml/1 tsp

Grind two-thirds of the oats in a blender or grinder. Mix with the buttermilk and leave to stand for 2 hours. Combine the yeast with 5ml/1tsp flour and 45ml/3tbsp tepid water. Leave for 10 minutes to activate. Combine the flour and yeast mixture with the ground oats,

the remaining oats, the butter, salt, chopped herbs, and caraway seeds. Mix to make a compact dough. Leave to rise, covered, in a warm place for 30–40 minutes.

Knead the dough well, then divide into three equal parts.

Sprinkle a worktop with flour and roll out into three strands, then plait into a braid.

Place on a floured baking sheet, cover and leave to rise for 30 minutes. Bake in an oven preheated to 220°C/425°F/Gas 7 for 30 minutes.

Mix the yolks with a little water. Shortly before the bread is cooked, brush it with the yolks and sprinkle with aniseed, caraway seeds and crushed or ground cardamom.

Remove from the oven, cool and serve with the Italian Cheese Pickle.

Tip

Aniseed can be replaced with either poppy or sesame seeds.

Sweet and Sour Spinach Ravioli

Ingredients Metric/Imperial

For the pastry:

Finely ground wholewheat flour	400g/14oz
Eggs, beaten	4/4
Sea salt	5g/1 tsp
Olive oil	15–30 ml/1–2 tbsp
Milk	30ml/2 tbsp
Eggs, separated	2/2
Fresh spinach, cooked or frozen spinach, thawed	450 g/1 lb
Onion, chopped	1 medium/1 medium
Breadcrumbs	45–60 g/3–4 tbsp
Sea salt to taste	
Freshly ground black pepper to taste	

For the sauce:

Onions, chopped	2/2
Chives, snipped	30ml/2 tbsp
Parsley, chopped	15ml/1 tbsp
Tarragon, chopped	15ml/1 tbsp
Hard-boiled (Hard-cooked) eggs	2/2
Cider vinegar	30ml/2 tbsp
Vegetable stock	225ml/8 fl oz
Olive oil	30ml/2 tbsp
Mustard	15ml/1 tbsp
Lemon	1/2/1/2
Orange marmalade	15 ml/1 tbsp

Sieve the flour on to a large wooden board and make a well in the centre. Add the eggs and combine with the salt and oil to make a smooth pastry. Add some milk if necessary. Cover and leave to stand in a warm place for at least 30 minutes. Roll out thinly on a floured worktop, cover again and leave to stand for 15 minutes.

In the meantime, separate the eggs and combine the yolks with the spinach, onion, breadcrumbs, salt and pepper.

Cut the pastry into small squares, and cover half of them with spinach. Brush the edges with lightly whisked egg white, then cover with the remaining squares. Be sure to press the edges firmly together.

Boil the filled pasta in salted water for 10–15 minutes, remove, drain well and keep warm.

To make the sauce, combine the chopped eggs with the herbs and onion. Pour the vinegar, stock, oil, mustard, lemon juice and marmalade on top, mix well then season to taste with salt and pepper.

Arrange the spinach pasta on plates, pour the sauce on top and serve.

Ratatouille Pie with Cheese Sauce

Ingredients

Ingredients	Metric/Imperial
Butter or margarine	45ml/3 tbsp
Spanish onion	1 medium/1 medium
Courgette (Zucchini)	1/1
Cucumber	1 small/1 small
Beef (steak) tomatoes, peeled and seeded	2 large/2 large
Aubergine (Eggplant)	1/1
Sea salt to taste	
Oregano, chopped	30ml/2 tbsp
Chives, snipped	30ml/2 tbsp
Freshly ground black pepper to taste	

For the sauce:

Butter or margarine	45ml/3 tbsp
Wholewheat flour	45–60 ml/3–4 tbsp
Milk	1/2l/18 fl oz
Ground nutmeg	a pinch/a pinch
Grated Parmesan cheese	50g/2oz

Additionally:

Mozzarella cheese	125 g/4 1/2 oz

Grease an ovenproof dish. Slice the onion, courgette, cucumber and tomatoes. Slice the aubergine and sprinkle with salt. Leave for 30 minutes then rinse and pat dry.

Arrange the vegetables in layers in the dish. Sprinkle each layer with herbs, salt and pepper.

For the sauce, heat the butter or margarine in a pan and stir in the flour. Add the milk, stirring constantly. Bring the sauce to the boil and stir until it is smooth and creamy. Season with the salt, pepper and nutmeg.

Pour the sauce over the vegetables, then cover with the sliced Mozzarella. Sprinkle with Parmesan.

Bake for 20–30 minutes in an oven preheated to 200°C/400°F/Gas 6. Remove and serve immediately.

Tip

You can of course use other vegetables for this dish, for instance cauliflower and broccoli. Firm vegetables should, however, be parboiled before baking.

Mushroom Turnovers

Ingredients — Metric/Imperial

Frozen puff pastry	450g/1lb

For the stuffing:

Butter or margarine	30ml/2 tbsp
Onion, chopped	1 medium/1 medium
Mushrooms, sliced	350g/12oz
Chives, snipped	15ml/1 tbsp
Parsley, chopped	15ml/1 tbsp
Watercress, chopped	1 bunch/1 bunch
Eggs	3/3
Sea salt to taste	
Freshly ground pepper to taste	
Nutmeg, ground	a pinch/a pinch

Additionally:

Egg yolk	1/1
Grated Parmesan cheese	50g/2oz

Roll out the defrosted pastry on a floured worktop.

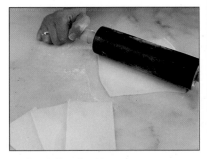

Heat the butter or margarine in a pan and gently sauté the onion until translucent. Add the mushrooms and fry for 1-2 minutes. Stir in the herbs.

Beat the eggs, season with salt, pepper and nutmeg. Pour over the mushrooms and cook until set, stirring constantly. Remove from the heat and leave to cool.

Spread the mushroom mixture on the pastry, fold over and firmly press the edges together. Place on to a

baking tray sprinkled with water and bake for 20 minutes in an oven preheated to 200°C/400°F/Gas 6.

Shortly before the time

up, brush the pastry with the egg yolk, combined with a little water, and sprinkle with Parmesan.

Remove and serve either hot or cold.

Tip

Any type of fresh or dried mushrooms available can be used for this dish. Delicatessens, health-food shops and supermarkets stock a wide range, although some do tend to be expensive.

Phyllo pastry can be used instead of puff pastry and does not have to be defrosted or rolled. It should be handled carefully, however, as it is very thin and tears easily.

Baked Apple Stuffed with Walnuts

Ingredients	Metric/Imperial
Cooking apples	4/4
Juice of lemon	1/1
Butter or margarine	30ml/2 tbsp
Walnuts	100g/4oz
Raisins, soaked	30ml/2 tbsp
Emmenthal or cheddar cheese, grated	50g/2oz
Sea salt to taste	
Freshly ground pepper to taste	

Additionally:

Oil for greasing	
Dry white wine	225ml/8 fl oz
Cress	1 box/1 box
Tarragon vinegar or lemon juice	15ml/1 tbsp

Wash and halve the apples, remove the core and sprinkle with lemon juice.

Combine the butter or margarine with the chopped nuts, raisins and cheese, then season with salt and pepper. Cover the apple halves with this mixture.

Grease an ovenproof dish and place the apples in it. Bake for 15 minutes in an oven preheated to 220°C/425°F/Gas 7

Pour the wine on top and bake for 5 minutes longer.

Remove from the oven, arrange on a plate and garnish with cress. Sprinkle vinegar or lemon juice over the cress and serve immediately.

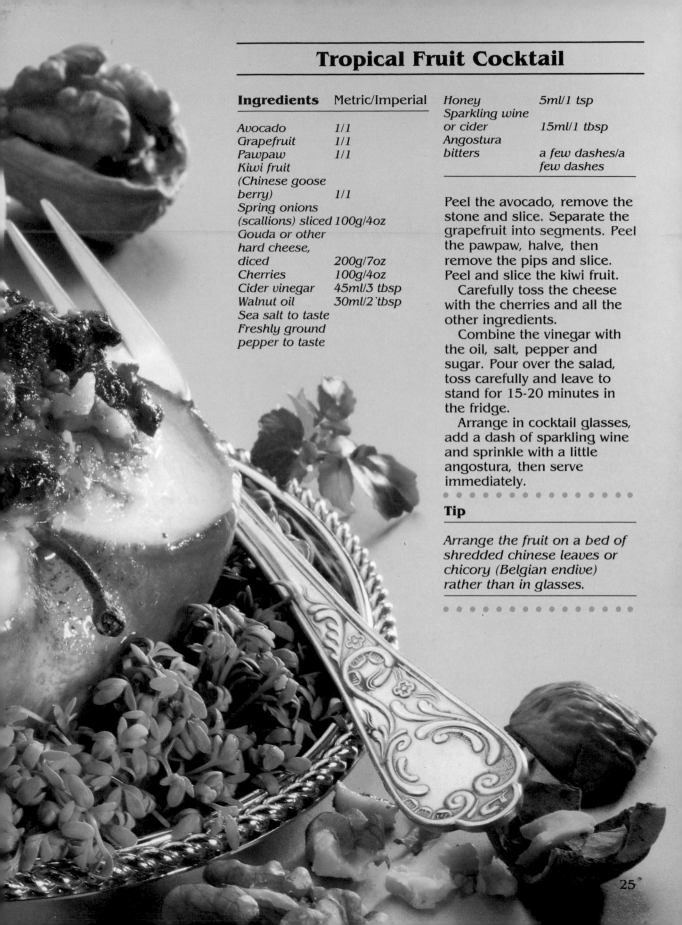

Tropical Fruit Cocktail

Ingredients	Metric/Imperial
Avocado	1/1
Grapefruit	1/1
Pawpaw	1/1
Kiwi fruit (Chinese goose berry)	1/1
Spring onions (scallions) sliced	100g/4oz
Gouda or other hard cheese, diced	200g/7oz
Cherries	100g/4oz
Cider vinegar	45ml/3 tbsp
Walnut oil	30ml/2 tbsp
Sea salt to taste	
Freshly ground pepper to taste	
Honey	5ml/1 tsp
Sparkling wine or cider	15ml/1 tbsp
Angostura bitters	a few dashes/a few dashes

Peel the avocado, remove the stone and slice. Separate the grapefruit into segments. Peel the pawpaw, halve, then remove the pips and slice. Peel and slice the kiwi fruit.

Carefully toss the cheese with the cherries and all the other ingredients.

Combine the vinegar with the oil, salt, pepper and sugar. Pour over the salad, toss carefully and leave to stand for 15-20 minutes in the fridge.

Arrange in cocktail glasses, add a dash of sparkling wine and sprinkle with a little angostura, then serve immediately.

Tip

Arrange the fruit on a bed of shredded chinese leaves or chicory (Belgian endive) rather than in glasses.

25

Medley of Vegetable Fritters

Ingredients Metric/Imperial

Broccoli florets,
separated   200g/7oz
Cauliflower
florets,
separated   200g/7oz
Carrots, cubed   200g/7oz
Celeriac, cubed 200g/7oz

For the batter:

Wholewheat
flour   125g/4½ oz
Beer   225 ml/8 fl oz
Olive oil   15 ml/1 tbsp
Sugar   5 ml/1 tsp
Salt   a pinch/a pinch
Egg yolk   1/1
Egg white   1/1
Oil for frying

For the sauce:

Tomatoes,
peeled, seeded
and chopped   4/4
Butter or
margarine   30 ml/2 tbsp
Onion, chopped 1/1
Tomato purée   30 ml/2 tbsp
Wholewheat
flour   30 ml/2 tbsp
White wine   225 ml/8 fl oz
Vegetable stock 225 ml/8fl oz
Single cream
(Light cream)   225 ml/8 fl oz
Salt to taste
Freshly ground
pepper to taste
Sugar   a pinch/a pinch
Oregano,
chopped   15 ml/1 tbsp

Wash the vegetables and
blanch in boiling salted water
for 5–10 minutes. Drain well.

For the batter, combine the
flour with the beer, oil, sugar,
salt and egg yolk and stir
well. Leave to stand for at
least 15 minutes.

Beat the egg whites until
they form stiff peaks and fold
in to the batter. Turn the
vegetables in the batter and
shallow fry in the oil until

golden brown. Drain well and
keep warm.

To make the sauce, sauté
the onions and tomatoes in
melted butter or margarine
for 5 minutes.

Stir in the tomato purée,
dust with flour, then pour in
the wine, stirring constantly,
and add the stock. Cover and
leave to simmer over medium
heat for 5 minutes, stirring
frequently.

Add the cream, season
with salt, pepper and sugar
and leave to simmer for a
further 5 minutes.

Add the oregano to the
sauce. Pour on to individual
plates, arrange the vegetable
pieces on top and serve
immediately.

Tomato Angelo

Ingredients   Metric/Imperial

Tomatoes, large	4×100 g/4×4 oz
Sea salt to taste	
Freshly ground pepper to taste	

For the stuffing:

Cream cheese	150g/5oz
Crème fraîche	30 ml/2 tbsp
Garlic clove, chopped	1/1
Salt	$2\frac{1}{2}$ ml/$\frac{1}{2}$ tsp
Chives, snipped	30 ml/2 tbsp
Parsley, chopped	30 ml/2 tbsp
Lemon balm, chopped	30 ml/2 tbsp
Cress, chopped	30 ml/2 tbsp
Lemon	$\frac{1}{2}$/$\frac{1}{2}$
Worcester sauce	a few drops/a few drops

Additionally:

Radicchio	1 small head/1 small head
Chicory (Endive)	2 small/2 small
Raspberry vinegar	a few drops/a few drops
Olive oil	a few drops/a few drops

Cut a lid off the tomatoes and remove the seeds with a spoon. Place upside down on a rack and leave to drain. Sprinkle with salt and pepper.

For the stuffing, combine the cream cheese with the crème fraîche, the garlic clove rubbed with salt, the herbs and the lemon juice to make a smooth mixture. Season to taste with salt, pepper and Worcester sauce. Fill the tomatoes with this mixture.

Wash the radicchio and chicory and cut into thin slices.

Arrange the salad on a plate, sprinkle with vinegar and oil, salt and pepper. Place the stuffed tomatoes on top and serve.

Soups

A light vegetable soup can replace the starter or can form the second course in a vegetarian dinner. However, hearty stews with potatoes, soya meat or pulses make a more complete meal. Vegetarian soups are formulated with a view to blending nutrients to achieve a well-balanced diet.

Spring Vegetable Soup

Ingredients

	Metric/Imperial
Butter or margarine	30 ml/2 tbsp
Onion, chopped	1/1
Young peas	100g/4oz
Carrots, cubed	2 small/2 small
Celeriac, cubed	½ small/½ small
Leek, sliced	1/1
Cucumber, cubed	½ small/½ small
White wine	225 ml/8 fl oz
Vegetable stock*	600 ml/1 pt
Butter or margarine	40g/1½oz
Wholewheat flour	40g/1½oz
Crème fraîche	60 ml/4 tbsp
Sea salt to taste	
Freshly ground pepper to taste	
Nutmeg	a pinch/a pinch
Chives, snipped	30 ml/2 tbsp

Heat the butter or margarine, then sauté the onion until translucent. Add the other vegetables and cook 3–4 minutes longer. Add the wine and stock, cover and simmer

over a medium heat for 8–10 minutes.

In the meantime, combine the butter or margarine and the flour to make a smooth paste.

Add the flour and butter mixture to the soup and simmer for a further 10 minutes.

Stir in the crème fraîche,

season with salt, pepper and nutmeg.

Serve the soup garnished with chives.

Tip

*To make vegetable stock, either combine a crumbled vegetable stock cube with sufficient boiling water to make 600 ml/1 pt or make homemade stock by combining ¼ cabbage with 1 onion, leek, carrot, celery stalk and bouquet garni in a large pan. Cover with 900 ml/1½ pts water and 15 ml/1 tbsp soya sauce, boil for 40 minutes and strain before using wherever vegetable stock is required. A large quantity of stock can be made at once and frozen in an ice cube tray to be used whenever needed.

Delicious Carrot Soup

Ingredients	Metric/Imperial
Carrots	600g/1½ lb
Butter or margarine	45 ml/3 tbsp
Vegetable stock	600 ml/1 pt
Sea salt to taste	
Freshly ground pepper to taste	
Sugar	a pinch/a pinch
Chervil, chopped	30 ml/2 tbsp
Sparkling wine	30 ml/2 tbsp
Single cream (Light cream)	100 ml/4 fl oz

Peel the carrots and cut them into small pieces, then fry gently in butter or margarine until translucent.

Pour in the stock, bring to the boil and cook for 30 minutes. Cool then purée in a food processor. Return the soup to the pan, reheat and season to taste with salt, pepper and sugar.

Stir in the chervil, then add a splash of sparkling wine. Remove from the heat and fold in the cream.

Pour into individual bowls and serve immediately.

Tip

You can replace the carrots with pumpkin to make this exquisite soup.

Wild Herb Soup

Ingredients — Metric/Imperial

Ingredients	Metric/Imperial
Spinach	250g/9oz
Young stinging nettles	100g/4oz
Sorrel	50g/2oz
Lettuce	1 medium/1 medium
Butter or margarine	30 ml/2 tbsp
Onion, chopped	1/1
Vegetable stock	400 ml/14 fl oz
Sea salt to taste	
Freshly ground pepper to taste	
Nutmeg	a pinch/a pinch
Single cream (Light cream)	100 ml/4 fl oz
Egg yolks, beaten	4/4

Additionally:

Wholewheat bread	4 slices/4 slices
Butter or margarine	60 ml/4 tbsp

Wash the spinach, stinging nettles, sorrel and lettuce thoroughly, then chop finely.

Heat the butter or margarine in a pan and gently fry the chopped onion until translucent. Add the vegetables, then pour in the stock. Bring to the boil and simmer for 15 minutes. Season with salt, pepper and nutmeg. Cool slightly and purée in a food processor. Return to the pan and reheat.

Whisk the cream with the yolks until smooth. Remove the soup from the heat and stir in the cream.

Cut the bread into small cubes, toast in the butter or margarine until golden brown, sprinkle on top of the soup and serve.

Bavarian Kohlrabi Soup

Pour in the wine, then add the tomatoes and stock. Bring to the boil, then season

Ingredients	Metric/Imperial
Kohlrabi	2 medium/2 medium
Butter or margarine	30 ml/2 tbsp
Onion, chopped	1 medium/1 medium
White wine	225 ml/8 fl oz
Tomatoes, peeled, seeded and chopped	4/4
Vegetable stock	400 ml/14 fl oz
Sea salt to taste	
Freshly ground pepper to taste	
Paprika	5 ml/1 tsp
Curry powder	5 ml/1 tsp
Oregano, chopped	5 ml/1 tsp
Mushrooms, sliced	225g/8oz

Watercress, chopped	1 bunch/1 bunch
Stuffed olives	8/8
Chopped walnuts	50g/2oz
Crème fraîche	225g/8oz

Peel the kohlrabi, then cut into small strips. Heat the butter or margarine in a pan and gently fry the onion and kohlrabi until translucent.

to taste with salt, pepper, paprika, curry powder and oregano. Simmer, covered, for 8–10 minutes.

Add the mushrooms to the soup.

• • • • • • • • • • • • •

Add the watercress, sliced olives and walnuts, bring to the boil once more, transfer into individual bowls and stir in some crème fraîche.

• • • • • • • • • • • • •

Chunky Vegetable Soup

Ingredients	Metric/Imperial
Butter or margarine	60 ml/4 tbsp
Spring onions (Scallions), sliced	100g/4 oz
Red pepper, seeded and sliced	1/1
Green pepper, seeded and sliced	1/1
Courgette (Zucchini)	1/1
Celery stalks, diced	2–3/2–3
Tomato pùree	30 ml/2 tbsp
Tomatoes, peeled, seeded and chopped	4/4
Vegetable stock	750 ml/1¼ pt
Worcester sauce	30 ml/2 tbsp
Sea salt to taste	
Freshly ground pepper to taste	
Honey	15 ml/1 tbsp
Basil, chopped	5 ml/1 tsp
Oregano, chopped	5 ml/1 tsp
Garlic cloves	2/2
Salt	5 ml/1 tsp
Tabasco (Hot pepper sauce) or 1 sliced chilli	a few drops
Pasta (for soups) or vermicelli	200g/7oz

Heat the butter or margarine

in a pan and sauté the spring onions until translucent. Add the peppers, sliced courgette and celery. Sauté briefly. Stir in the tomato purée, and tomatoes.

Pour in the stock and Worcester sauce, then season with salt, pepper, sugar, chopped herbs and the garlic crushed with salt.

Cover and leave to simmer over a medium heat for 15 minutes.

Season to taste, add a few drops of Tabasco, add the boiled pasta to the soup and serve.

Peking Soup

Ingredients	Metric/Imperial
Sesame oil	45 ml/3 tbsp
Spring onions (Scallions), sliced	100g/4oz
Red pepper, seeded and sliced	1/1
Carrot, sliced	1/1
Celeriac, sliced	1/2/1/2
Soya bean sprouts	150g/5oz
Chinese mushrooms, soaked	100g/4oz
Garlic cloves	2/2
Sea salt	5 ml/1 tsp
Soya sauce	30 ml/2 tbsp
Cider vinegar	30 ml/2 tbsp
Honey	30 ml/2 tbsp
Vegetable stock	750 ml/1¼ pt
Dry sherry	100 ml/4 fl oz
Wild rice and/or brown rice, boiled	200g/7oz
Sea salt to taste	
Freshly ground pepper to taste	
Chives, snipped	30 ml/2 tbsp
Egg, hard-boiled (hard-cooked)	1/1

Heat the oil in a pan, then fry vegetables until brown. Add the bean sprouts and the finely sliced mushrooms and sauté briefly. Crush the garlic with the salt, add to the vegetables, then season with soya sauce, vinegar and honey.

Pour in the stock, cover and leave to boil over a medium heat for 8–10 minutes.

Flavour with sherry, then add the rice to the soup. Season to taste with salt and pepper.

Transfer the soup to a terrine or several individual bowls and serve sprinkled with chives and chopped egg.

● ● ● ● ● ● ● ● ● ● ● ●
Tip

If possible, use fresh bean sprouts. You can buy them or grow them yourself from dried soya beans.

● ● ● ● ● ● ● ● ● ● ● ●

Brittany Soup

Ingredients

Ingredients	Metric/Imperial
Butter or margarine	45 ml/3 tbsp
Onions, chopped	2 medium/2 medium
Carrots	2/2
Potatoes, large	2/2
Haricot beans (Navy beans)	250g/9oz
Tomato purée	30 ml/2 tbsp
White wine	225 ml/8 fl oz
Vegetable stock	750 ml/1¼ pt
Sea salt to taste	
Freshly ground pepper to taste	
Ground caraway	a pinch/a pinch
Marjoram, chopped	5 ml/1 tsp
White beans, tinned	100g/4oz
Tofu, cubed	100g/4oz
Cornflour (Corn starch)	15–30 ml/1–2 tbsp
Crème fraîche	225g/8oz
Tomatoes, skinned, seeded and chopped	2/2
Grated Parmesan cheese	100g/4oz
Chives, snipped	15 ml/1 tbsp

Heat the butter or margarine in a pan and sauté the onion until translucent.

Dice the peeled potatoes and carrots and add to the onions with the sliced beans. Sauté briefly.

Stir in the tomato purée, then pour in the wine and top up with stock. Cover and simmer over medium heat for about 15 minutes.

Season with salt, pepper, ground caraway and marjoram.

Add the drained white beans and the diced tofu and heat for approximately 4 minutes. Mix the cornflour with the cream until smooth and thicken the soup with it.

Add the tomatoes and Parmesan to the soup.

Season to taste, transfer to a terrine, sprinkle with chives and serve.

Beetroot and Tofu Soup

Ingredients	Metric/Imperial
Sesame oil	45 ml/3 tbsp
Tofu, diced	150g/5oz
Onion, chopped	1/1
Leek, sliced	1 small/ 1 small
Beetroot (Beet), grated	1 medium/1 medium
Vegetable stock	½ l/18 fl oz
Peas	150g/5oz
Sweetcorn (Corn kernels)	100g/4oz
Cucumber	1 small/1 small
Single cream (Light cream)	100 ml/4 fl oz
Crème fraîche	100g/4oz
Cornflour (Cornstarch)	15–30 ml/1–2 tbsp
Sea salt to taste	
Freshly ground pepper to taste	
Ground caraway	5 ml/1 tsp
Sugar	a pinch/a pinch
Capers	15 ml/1 tbsp
Chives, snipped	30 ml/2 tbsp

Heat the oil in a pan and fry the tofu. Add the onion and leek. Fry until translucent.

Stir in the beetroot and peas. Continue to sauté, stirring constantly.

Pour in the stock and simmer for 10 minutes.

Drain the sweetcorn and add to the soup with the diced cucumber, cream and crème fraîche. Simmer a further 5 minutes.

Mix the cornflour with a little water and thicken the

soup with it, then season with salt, pepper, caraway and sugar.

Stir the capers into the soup, heat thoroughly serve sprinkled with chives.

Herb Ravioli in Broth

Ingredients	Metric/Imperial

For the pastry:

Flour, plain (all-purpose)	225g/8oz
Egg, beaten	1/1
Oil	15 ml/1 tbsp
Water	225ml/8fl oz
Sea salt	a pinch/a pinch

For the stuffing:

Butter or margarine	30ml/2 tbsp
Spring onions (Scallions), sliced	100g/4oz
Parsley, chopped	30ml/2 tbsp
Chives, snipped	30ml/2 tbsp
Toasted cubes of wholewheat bread	150g/5oz
Eggs, beaten	2/2
Sea salt to taste	
Freshly ground pepper to taste	
Nutmeg	a pinch/a pinch

Additionally:

Egg yolks	2/2
Vegetable stock	1 l/1¾ pt

Combine the flour with the egg, oil, water and salt to make a firm pastry. Leave in the fridge for at least 30 minutes.

In the meantime, heat the butter or margarine and gently fry the spring onions until translucent. Stir in the herbs and bread cubes. Add the eggs, season mixture with salt, pepper and nutmeg and stir until the egg has set.

Roll out the pastry on a floured worktop and cut into squares or rectangles. Cover half the pastry squares with the egg mixture.

Brush the edges of the pastry with egg yolk, place the remaining squares on top and press the edges firmly together. Simmer in the stock

for about 10 minutes or until done.

Drain the ravioli, transfer to bowls, pour a little stock on top and serve.

41

Love Apple Soup

Ingredients Metric/Imperial

For the soup:

Ripe tomatoes peeled, seeded and chopped	600g/1 1/2lb
Butter or margarine	30ml/2 tbsp
Onion, chopped	1 large/1 large
Tomato purée	30ml/2 tbsp
Wholewheat flour	15ml/1 tbsp
Vegetable stock	600ml/1pt
Crème fraîche	225g/8oz
Sea salt to taste	
Freshly ground pepper to taste	
Mint, chopped	30ml/2 tbsp

For the semolina dumplings:

Butter	60g/2 1/2oz
Egg, beaten	1/1
Semolina	100g/4oz
Sea salt to taste	
Freshly ground white pepper to taste	
Oil	

Additionally:

Chives, snipped	30ml/2 tbsp

Heat the butter or margarine and sauté the onion until translucent. Add the tomatoes, stir in the tomato purée, sprinkle with flour, then pour in the stock, stirring constantly. Leave to simmer over medium heat for 10–15 minutes. Cool slightly then press the soup through a fine sieve or purée in a food processor.

Reheat in a pan, stir in the crème fraîche, season with salt, pepper and mint.

To make the dumplings, cream the butter, add the beaten egg and blend in the semolina. Season with salt and pepper and leave,

covered, for about 10 minutes.

With a teaspoon, make even-shaped dumplings from the mixture. Place on to an oiled plate and leave in the

fridge for a further 20 minutes.

Simmer carefully in boiling salted water for 10 minutes.

Pour the tomato soup in to a terrine and gently transfer the dumplings from the water to the soup, draining them well. Sprinkle with chives and serve immediately.

• • • • • • • • • • • • • • • •

Tip

You can use these semolina dumplings in any other vegetable soup.

• • • • • • • • • • • • • • • •

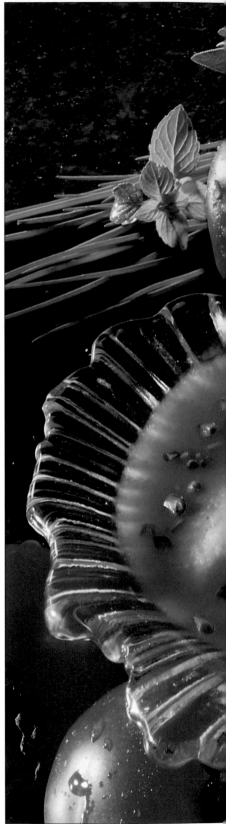

Orange and Vegetable Soup

Ingredients	Metric/Imperial
Sesame oil	30ml/2 tbsp
Onion, chopped	1/1
Leek, sliced	1 small/1 small
Carrots, sliced	2/2
Red pepper, seeded and sliced	1/1
Green pepper, seeded and sliced	1/1
Chinese leaves	1 small head/1 small head
Oranges	2/2
Grapefruit	2/2
Vegetable stock	1 l/1¾pt
Sea salt to taste	
Freshly ground pepper to taste	
Nutmeg	a pinch/a pinch
Ground ginger	a pinch/a pinch
Caraway seeds	5ml/1 tsp
Honey	2½ml/½ tsp
Parsley, chopped	15ml/1 tbsp
Chives, snipped	15ml/1 tbsp

Heat the oil in a pan and sauté the onion until translucent.

Add the leek, carrots, and peppers to the onion. Fry gently.

Quarter the Chinese leaves, remove the stem and cut into fine strips. Add to the vegetables and gently fry for a short while.

Peel the oranges and grapefruit, then separate into segments. Add to the vegetables, and pour the stock on top.

Season with salt, pepper, nutmeg, ginger, caraway and honey. Simmer over a medium heat for 15 minutes.

Season to taste and serve sprinkled with herbs.

Chinese Egg and Mushroom Soup

Ingredients	Metric/Imperial
Sesame oil	30ml/2 tbsp
Onion, sliced	1/1
Carrot, sliced	1/1
Leek, sliced	1 small/1 small
Chinese mushrooms, soaked and sliced	100g/4oz
Vegetable stock	750ml/1¼ pt
Soya sauce	30ml/2 tbsp
Ground ginger	a pinch/a pinch
Sea salt to taste	
Freshly ground pepper to taste	
Sugar	a pinch/a pinch
Sherry	100ml/4fl oz
Egg whites	4/4
Egg yolks	4/4
Chives, snipped	30ml/2 tbsp

Heat the oil and sauté the onion until translucent.

Add the carrots, leeks and mushrooms. Sauté briefly.

Pour in the stock, season with soya sauce, ginger, salt, pepper and sugar and

simmer, covered, for 5 minutes.

Stir in the sherry. Whisk the egg whites and pour through a strainer into the soup. Simmer for a further 5 minutes.

Transfer the soup in to four individual bowls. Garnish each with an egg yolk and sprinkle with chives.

Mimi's Lettuce Soup

Ingredients	Metric/Imperial
Butter or margarine	30ml/2 tbsp
Onion, chopped	1 medium/ 1 medium
Lettuce	1/1
Vegetable stock	750ml/1¼pt
Sea salt to taste	
Freshly ground pepper to taste	
Nutmeg	a pinch/a pinch
Single cream (light cream)	100ml/4fl oz

Additionally:

Vinegar	15ml/1 tbsp
Water	½l/18fl oz
Eggs	4/4
Chervil, chopped	30ml/2 tbsp

Heat the butter or margarine in a pan and gently fry the onion. Add the washed and torn up lettuce leaves.

Pour in the stock and cook for 15 minutes. Cool slightly. Purée in a food processor.

Reheat in a pan, season to taste with salt, pepper and nutmeg and add the cream.

Bring the vinegar and water to the boil. Poach the eggs then drain well.

Transfer the soup to individual bowls, add an egg to each and serve sprinkled with chervil.

45

Main Dishes

The main dishes in a vegetarian dinner generally consist of vegetables combined with cereals, soya or pulses, thereby providing all the required nutrients in well-balanced proportions. Try our bakes, ragouts and herbed roasts — you'll be amazed at how varied and tasty vegetarian dishes are!

Pepperoni Aux Herbes de Provence

Ingredients

Ingredients	Metric/Imperial
Peppers	4 medium/4 medium
Onions, chopped	2/2
Mushrooms, chopped	225g/8oz
Eggs, beaten	2–3/2–3
Grated Emmental cheese	100g/4oz
Breadcrumbs	30–45ml/2–3 tbsp
Parsley, chopped	30ml/2 tbsp
Sea salt to taste	
Freshly ground pepper to taste	
Nutmeg	a pinch/a pinch

Additionally:

Tomatoes, peeled, seeded and chopped	4/4
Crème fraîche	225g/8oz
White wine	225ml/8fl oz
Herbes de Provence (Basil; Rosemary — garlic as preferred)	15ml/1 tbsp

Cut a lid off each pepper, remove the seeds then wash the peppers and drain well.

Combine the eggs, onions, mushrooms, Emmental and breadcrumbs. Add the herbs then season with salt, pepper and nutmeg. Fill the peppers with this mixture and place them close together in an oven-proof dish.

Combine the tomatoes, crème fraîche and wine. Season with herbs then pour over and around the peppers.

Bake for 20 minutes in an oven preheated to 200°C/400°F/Gas 6. Serve immediately.

Tip

You can also stuff tomatoes, Spanish onions or aubergines in this way.

Soya Risotto

Ingredients Metric/Imperial

	Metric/Imperial
Butter or margarine	50g/2oz
Onion, chopped	1/1
Carrots, diced	2/2
Celeriac, diced	½/½
Leek, sliced	1 small/1 small
Courgette (zucchini) diced	1/1
White wine	225ml/8fl oz
Lemon	1/1
Worcester sauce	a few dashes/ a few dashes
Soya sausages (made with soya grits and eggs)	8 small/8 small
Brown rice	250g/9oz
Vegetable stock	1 l/1¾pt
Sea salt to taste	
Freshly ground pepper to taste	
Tomatoes, peeled, seeded and chopped	4/4
Crème fraîche	225g/8oz
Chives, snipped	30ml/2 tbsp

Heat the butter or margarine in a pan and sauté the vegetables until translucent. Pour in the wine, then season with lemon juice and Worcester sauce. Cover and simmer for 5 minutes.

Add the sliced sausages and the rice and sauté briefly.

Pour in two cups of stock and leave to boil over medium heat, uncovered.

Stir occasionally, gradually adding the remaining stock. The risotto will be ready in approximately 30–40 minutes.

Season with salt and pepper and add the tomatoes and crème fraîche. Serve sprinkled with chives.

Tip

You can prepare the risotto without the sausages and serve them separately.

Spinach and Herb Loaf

Ingredients	Metric/Imperial
Butter or margarine	30ml/2 tbsp
Onion, chopped	1 medium/1 medium
Spinach, fresh or frozen	500g/1lb
Bread rolls	8/8
Vegetable stock	300ml/10fl oz
Parsley, chopped	15ml/1 tbsp
Chives, snipped	15ml/1 tbsp
Chervil chopped	15ml/1 tbsp
Tarragon, chopped	15ml/1 tbsp
Garlic cloves	2/2
Sea salt	5ml/1 tsp
Crème fraîche	225g/8oz
Eggs, beaten	4/4
Wholewheat flour	30–45ml/2–3 tbsp
Breadcrumbs	30–45ml/2–3 tbsp
Oil for greasing	

Heat the butter or margarine and gently fry the onion until translucent. Wash the spinach, if it is fresh or defrost if it is frozen. Add to the onion and sauté briefly.

Crumble the rolls into the stock. Crush the garlic with salt.

Add the spinach, herbs and garlic to the stock. Fold in the crème fraîche, eggs, flour and breadcrumbs. Knead well to make a compact mixture.

Grease an oven-proof dish, transfer the spinach loaf into it, then bake for 40–45 minutes in an oven preheated to 220°C/425°F/Gas 7.

• • • • • • • • • • • • • • •

Tip

You can serve a tomato or cheese sauce with this 'roast'.

• • • • • • • • • • • • • • •

Pancakes 'Four Season'

Ingredients   Metric/Imperial

For the batter:

Wholewheat flour	100g/4oz
Milk	225ml/8fl oz
Eggs, beaten	4/4
Salt	a pinch/a pinch
Olive oil	15ml/1 tbsp

Additionally:

Mushrooms, halved	125g/4½oz
Tomatoes, peeled, seeded and chopped	2/2
Cucumber	1 small/1 small
Sweetcorn (Corn kernels)	100g/4oz
Peas	100g/4oz
Sea salt to taste	
Freshly ground pepper to taste	
Oregano, chopped	15ml/1 tbsp
Mozzarella cheese, diced	125g/4½oz
Oil for frying	
Chives, snipped	30ml/2 tbsp

Whisk the flour with the milk, eggs, salt and oil to make a smooth batter, then leave to stand.

Peel, halve, seed and slice the cucumber.

Drain the sweetcorn. Blanch the peas for 5 minutes in salted water. Drain then combine all the vegetables. Season with salt, pepper and oregano.

For each serving, pour a quarter of the batter into a frying pan, bake, then cover with a quarter of the vegetables. Transfer to an oven-proof dish. Repeat with the remaining batter and vegetables.

Sprinkle the pancakes with Mozzarella, then bake in an oven preheated to 220°C/425°F/Gas 7 for 5–10 minutes.

Remove from the oven, sprinkle with chives and serve immediately.

Stuffed Aubergines

Ingredients	Metric/Imperial
Aubergines (Eggplants)	2 large/2 large
Olive oil	45ml/3 tbsp
Garlic cloves	2/2
Sea salt	5ml/1 tsp
Onion, chopped	1/1
Tomatoes, peeled, seeded and chopped	4/4
Vegetable stock	225ml/8fl oz

For the stuffing:

Soya granules	225g/8oz
Low-fat quark	150g/5oz
Tomato purée	30ml/2 tbsp
Basil, chopped	5ml/1 tsp
Oregano, chopped	5 ml/1 tsp
Eggs, beaten	2/2
Chives, snipped	15ml/1 tbsp

Parsley, chopped	15ml/1 tbsp
Grated Emmenthal cheese	125g/4½oz
Salt to taste	
Freshly ground pepper to taste	

Halve the aubergines and parboil for 5 minutes in salted water. Drain well.

Crush the garlic with the salt. Sauté in hot oil with the onion. Add the tomatoes and the stock, cover, and simmer for 5 minutes.

Prepare the soya granules according to the instructions on the package. Add the quark, tomato purée, spices, eggs and herbs. Mix well. If necessary, bind the mixture with some breadcrumbs.

Add the Emmenthal, season with salt and pepper and leave for 20 minutes.

Fill the aubergines with this mixture and then place in an oven-proof dish. Pour over the tomato sauce and bake in an oven preheated to 200°C/400°F/Gas 6 for 15–20 minutes. Serve immediately.

Tip

You can use this stuffing for other kinds of vegetables, for instance courgettes, cucumbers or small pumpkins.

Soya dumplings in beer sauce

Ingredients	Metric/Imperial
Soya granules	225g/8oz
Vegetable stock	400ml/14fl oz
Low-fat quark	150g/5oz
Eggs, beaten	2/2
Peanut oil	30ml/2 tbsp
Mustard	15ml/1 tbsp
Marjoram, chopped	5ml/1 tsp
Garlic clove, chopped	1/1
Whisky	30ml/2 tbsp
Parsley, chopped	30ml/2 tbsp
Sea salt to taste	
Freshly ground pepper to taste	
Oil for deep-frying	

For the sauce:

Onion, chopped	1/1
Leek	1 small/1 small
Carrots	2/2
Celeriac	1/2/1/2
Olive oil	15ml/1 tbsp
Tomato purée	30ml/2 tbsp
Wholewheat flour	45ml/3 tbsp
Vegetable stock	300ml/10fl oz
Beer (flat and strong)	150ml/5fl oz
Honey	30ml/2 tbsp
Cider vinegar	30ml/2 tbsp
Marjoram	5ml/1 tbsp
Thyme	5ml/1 tbsp

Combine the soya granules with the stock. Add the quark, eggs, oil, mustard, marjoram, garlic, whisky and chopped parsley. Stir until smooth. If necessary, bind with breadcrumbs or flour. Season with salt and pepper.

Shape into little dumplings and deep-fry in hot oil. Drain well and keep warm.

To make the sauce, wash the vegetables and cut into thin strips. Heat the oil in a pan and sauté the vegetables until translucent. Stir in the tomato purée, dust with flour and pour in the stock and beer. Add the honey, vinegar, marjoram, thyme, salt and pepper. Simmer, covered, for 8–10 minutes.

Arrange the dumplings on serving dishes and pour the sauce on top. Serve immediately.

Vegetableburger

Ingredients	Metric/Imperial
Wholewheat rolls	4/4
Tartare sauce	60ml/4 tbsp
Lettuce leaves	
Radicchio leaves	
Tomato	1 large/1 large
Tofu, sliced	100g/4oz
Flour	
Egg, beaten	1/1
Golden breadcrumbs	50g/2oz
Oil for frying	
Spanish onion, sliced	1/1
Cress	1 box/1 box
Crème fraîche	50g/2oz
Mustard	30ml/2 tbsp
Sea salt to taste	
Freshly ground pepper to taste	
Soya sauce	15ml/1 tbsp
Sugar	2½ml/½ tsp

Halve the rolls and toast under the grill (broiler). Cover with tartare sauce, lettuce and radicchio leaves and sliced tomato.

Coat the tofu slices with flour, then dip in egg and breadcrumbs. Shallow fry on both sides until golden brown. Drain well. Place on top of the tomato. Garnish with onion and sprinkle with cress.

Combine the créme fraîche with the mustard, salt, pepper, soya sauce, and sugar. Spread over the burgers.

Cover with the other half of the roll before serving.

Tofu Ragout

Ingredients	Metric/Imperial
Tofu-Cauldron	250g/9oz
Vegetable stock	½l/18fl oz
Wholewheat flour	125g/5oz
Oil for frying	

Additionally:

Butter or margarine	30ml/2 tbsp
Onion, chopped	1/1
Green pepper, seeded and diced	1/1
Mushrooms, sliced	100g/4oz
White wine	225ml/8fl oz
Vegetable stock	225ml/8fl oz
Crème fraîche	100g/4oz
Cornflour (Cornstarch)	15ml/1 tbsp
Water	30ml/2 tbsp
Sea salt to taste	
Freshly ground pepper to taste	
Nutmeg	a pinch/a pinch
Soya sauce	a few dashes/a few dashes

Grated Parmesan cheese	50g/2oz
Parsley, chopped	30ml/2 tbsp

Cut the tofu into thin strips, transfer into the hot stock and leave for 15 minutes. Remove, drain well, turn in flour and fry in a little oil.

In the meantime, heat the butter or margarine and sauté the onion and pepper until translucent. Add the mushrooms, then pour in the wine and stock. Stir in the crème fraîche, then add the tofu. Simmer over a medium heat for 5–10 minutes.

Combine the cornflour and water. Stir in to the ragout to thicken slightly then season with salt, pepper, nutmeg and soya sauce.

Stir in Parmesan to taste, sprinkle with parsley and serve.

Hearty Country Hot Pot

Ingredients

Ingredients	Metric/Imperial
Soya cubes (dried)	150g/5oz
Vegetable stock	½l/18fl oz
Butter or margarine	60ml/4 tbsp
Onion, chopped	1/1
Leek, sliced	1/1
Carrots, cubed	2/2
Potatoes, cubed	4 large/4 large
Tomato purée	30ml/2 tbsp
Wholewheat flour	45ml/3 tbsp
Red wine	225ml/8fl oz
Marjoram, chopped	5ml/1 tsp
Thyme, chopped	5ml/1 tsp
Mushrooms	300g/10oz
Single cream (Light cream)	225ml/8fl oz
Blue cheese, crumbled	100g/4oz
Salt to taste	
Freshly ground pepper to taste	
Parsley, chopped	30ml/2 tbsp

Place the soya cubes into a bowl, pour the stock on top and leave for 30 minutes.

Heat the butter or margarine and gently fry the well-drained soya cubes. Add the vegetables and sauté briefly. Stir in the tomato purée, dust with flour then add the wine and the stock used for soaking the soya cubes. Season with marjoram and thyme and add the mushrooms. Simmer over a medium heat for 25–30 minutes.

Add the cream and the crumbled blue cheese, then season to taste with salt and pepper. Sprinkle with parsley and serve.

Hungarian Soya Goulash

Ingredients

Ingredients	Metric/Imperial
Soya cubes (dried)	150g/5oz
Vegetable stock	½l/18fl oz
Red wine	225ml/8fl oz
Olive oil	45ml/3 tbsp
Mushrooms, sliced	250g/9oz
Spanish onions, sliced	2/2
Red pepper, seeded and sliced	1/1
Green pepper, seeded and sliced	1/1
Tomato purée	30ml/2 tbsp
Wholewheat flour	30ml/2 tbsp
Tomatoes, peeled, seeded and chopped	2 large/2 large
Grated rind of lemon	15ml/1 tbsp
Sea salt	5ml/1 tsp
Garlic cloves	2/2
Ground caraway	5ml/1 tsp
Marjoram, chopped	15ml/1 tbsp
Paprika	5ml/1 tsp
Sea salt to taste	
Freshly ground pepper to taste	
Soured cream	225ml/8oz
Chives, snipped	30ml/2 tbsp

Cover the soya cubes with stock and wine and leave to soak for at least 30 minutes.

Heat the oil in a pan and briefly sauté the well-drained cubes. Add the onions, mushrooms and peppers.

Stir in the tomato purée, dust with flour, then add the tomatoes and the liquid from soaking the cubes.

Crush the garlic with salt. Add to the goulash along with the lemon rind, caraway, marjoram and paprika. Simmer over a medium heat for 25–30 minutes.

Season to taste with salt and pepper. Simmer for a further 5 minutes.

Transfer the goulash on to individual plates, garnish with a tablespoonful of cream each and sprinkle with chives.

Asparagus in White Wine Sauce

Ingredients	Metric/Imperial
Fresh asparagus	1½kg/3lb
Lemon	1/1
White wine	225ml/8fl oz
Water	½l/18fl oz
Salt	a pinch/a pinch
Butter	5ml/1 tsp

For the egg sauce:

Butter	125g/4½oz
Egg yolks	4/4
White wine	50ml/2fl oz
Lemon	1/1
Sea salt to taste	
Freshly ground pepper to taste	
Sugar	2½ml/½ tsp
Worcester sauce	a dash/a dash
Chervil, snipped	30ml/2 tbsp

Peel the asparagus, cut to equal lengths and tie together in bundles.

Bring the lemon juice, wine, water, salt and butter to the boil. Add the bundles of asparagus and cook for 15 minutes or until tender.

In the meantime, heat the butter in a pan.

Whisk the egg yolks with the wine and lemon juice in a different pan. Season with salt, pepper, sugar and Worcester sauce. Whisk in a double boiler until the mixture becomes creamy. Fold in the warm butter, drop by drop. Season the sauce to taste, then fold in the chervil.

Arrange the asparagus on a plate, pour over the sauce and serve immediately.

Tip

This light egg sauce also goes well with any other tender vegetables.

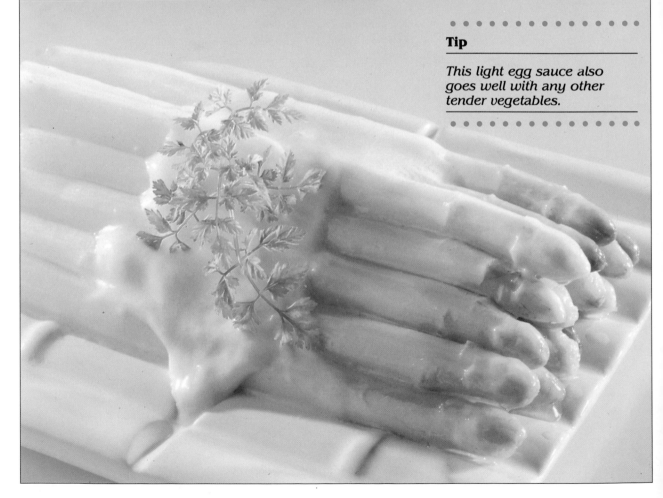

Amsterdam Egg Bake

Ingredients — Metric/Imperial

Ingredients	Metric/Imperial
Butter or margarine	30ml/2 tbsp
Onion, chopped	1/1
Spring onions (Scallions)	100g/4oz
Mushrooms, sliced	8–10/8–10
Fresh peaches	2/2
Tomatoes, peeled, seeded and sliced	4/4
Soured cream	225g/8oz
Grated Gouda cheese	150g/5oz
Sea salt to taste	
Freshly ground pepper to taste	
Nutmeg	a pinch/a pinch
Chives, snipped	30ml/2 tbsp

Additionally:

Hard-boiled eggs (Hard-cooked eggs)	6/6
Oil for greasing	

Heat the butter or margarine and gently fry the onion until translucent. Add the sliced spring onions and

mushrooms and sauté briefly.

Plunge the peaches into boiling water for 1 minute then remove and peel. Cut in half and remove the stone. Slice the fruit.

Combine the soured cream, Gouda, salt, pepper, nutmeg and chives.

Arrange the tomatoes, peaches and sautéed vegetables in layers in a greased oven-proof dish.

Place the peeled and sliced eggs on top. Pour over the sauce.

Bake for 10–15 minutes in an oven preheated to 200°C/400°F/Gas 6.

Vegetable Croquettes

Ingredients	Metric/Imperial
Butter or margarine	30ml/2 tbsp
Onion	1/1
Cooked peas	500g/1lb
Eggs, beaten	2/2
Mustard	15ml/1 tbsp
Rolls, soaked in water	2/2
Sea salt to taste	
Freshly ground pepper to taste	
Nutmeg	a pinch/a pinch
Soya sauce	15ml/1 tbsp
Parsley, chopped	30ml/2 tbsp
Green peppercorns	5ml/1 tsp
Rolled oats, for binding	30—45ml/2—3 tbsp

Swabian Lentils

Ingredients	Metric/Imperial
Lentils, soaked overnight	400g/14oz
Vegetable stock	½l/18fl oz
Butter or margarine	30ml/2 tbsp
Onion, chopped	1/1
Carrots, diced	2/2
Leek, sliced	1 small/1 small
Tomato purée	30ml/2 tbsp
White wine	225ml/8fl oz
Lemon	1/1
Crème fraîche	225g/8oz
Wholewheat flour	15—30ml/1—2 tbsp
Sea salt to taste	
Freshly ground pepper to taste	
Honey	30ml/2 tbsp
Cider vinegar	60ml/4 tbsp

Additionally:

Small pasta	200g/7oz
Oil for frying	
Nutmeg	a pinch/a pinch
Chives, snipped	30ml/2 tbsp

Rinse the lentils, then boil for 15—20 minutes in the stock.

In the meantime, heat the butter or margarine and gently fry the vegetables until translucent. Stir in the tomato purée, pour in the wine and lemon juice and add to the lentils. Combine the crème fraîche with the flour and stir into the lentils. Season to taste with salt, pepper, honey and vinegar.

Cook the pasta until tender, then fry with a little fat and season with salt, pepper and nutmeg.

Arrange on a plate, spread the lentils on top and garnish with chives.

Additionally:

Wholewheat flour	150g/5 oz
Eggs, beaten	2/2
Golden breadcrumbs	150g/5oz
Oil for frying	

Heat the butter or margarine and fry the onion until golden brown.

Purée the peas in a food processor or with a mixer.

Combine the onion, mashed peas, eggs, mustard and the well-squeezed rolls to make a compact mixture. Season to taste with salt, pepper, nutmeg and soya sauce.

Knead in the parsley and peppercorns. Bind with oats.

Shape the rissoles with your hands first dipped into water. Turn first in flour, then dip in eggs and breadcrumbs.

Fry in a little oil until golden brown, drain well and serve immediately.

Tip

You can also prepare these rissoles with chick peas, beans or lentils.

Pasta and Potatoes

Although pasta has been a staple of the Chinese and Italian diets for many centuries, new recommendations concerning healthy eating and the current economic recession have combined in recent years to increase the popularity of pasta dishes.

Home-made Wholewheat Pasta

Ingredients	Metric/Imperial
Freshly ground wholewheat flour	225g/8oz
Sea salt	a pinch/a pinch
Nutmeg	a pinch/a pinch
Eggs, beaten	2/2
Olive oil	15–30ml/1–2 tbsp
Water, if necessary	15–30ml/1–2 tbsp

Place the very finely ground flour in a bowl and mix with the salt and nutmeg. Combine with the eggs, oil and, if necessary, water to make a smooth dough. Cover with a moist cloth and leave for 30 minutes.

Roll out the dough very thinly and cut into the required shape. Boil the pasta in salted water for 5–10 minutes, according to size and shape.

• • • • • • • • • • • • • • • • •

Tip

You can colour the pasta by adding tomato purée, finely chopped herbs, saffron or mashed spinach to the dough.

• • • • • • • • • • • • • • • • •

Mushroom Sauce

Ingredients	Metric/Imperial
Butter or margarine	45ml/3 tbsp
Onions, chopped	2 small/2 small
Chanterelles, sliced	200g/7oz
Mushrooms, sliced	400g/14oz
Flour	30ml/2 tbsp
White wine	225ml/8fl oz
Vegetable stock	400ml/14fl oz
Sea salt	
Freshly ground pepper	
Single cream (Light cream)	225ml/8fl oz
Parsley, chopped	15ml/1 tbsp
Chives, snipped	15ml/1 tbsp
Chervil, chopped	15ml/1 tbsp

Heat the butter or margarine and sauté the onions until translucent. Add the chanterelles and mushrooms to the onions. Sauté briefly. Dust with flour then pour in the wine and stock. Simmer over medium heat for 8–10 minutes.

Season with salt and pepper. Add the cream.

Fold in the herbs, adjust the seasoning and serve.

Japanese Tofu Sauce

Ingredients	Metric/Imperial
Butter or margarine	30ml/2 tbsp
Tofu, diced	150g/5oz
Onion, chopped	1/1
Red pepper, seeded and diced	1/1
Green pepper, seeded and diced	1/1
Wholewheat flour	30ml/2 tbsp
Tomatoes, peeled, seeded and chopped	2/2
Gherkins, diced	2/2
Red wine	225ml/8fl oz
Vegetable stock	225ml/8fl oz
Salt to taste	
Freshly ground pepper to taste	
Paprika	5ml/1 tsp
Curry powder	2½ml/½ tsp
Crème fraîche	100g/4oz
Chives, snipped	30ml/2 tbsp

Heat the butter or margarine and briefly fry the tofu. Add the onion and diced peppers and sauté. Dust with flour, then add the tomatoes and gherkins. Pour in the wine and stock, cover and simmer over a medium heat for 10 minutes.

Season to taste with salt, pepper, paprika and curry powder.

• • • • • • • • • • • • • • •

Stir in the crème fraîche, pour the sauce over the cooked pasta and sprinkle with chives before serving.

• • • • • • • • • • • • • • •

67

Mushroom Crescents

Ingredients   Metric/Imperial

For the pastry:

Freshly ground wholewheat flour	300g/10oz
Sea salt	a pinch/a pinch
Water	225–450ml/8–16 fl oz

For the stuffing:

Butter or margarine	30ml/2 tbsp
Spring onions (Scallions), sliced	100g/4oz
Bean sprouts	150g/5oz
Chinese mushrooms, soaked and sliced	15g/½oz
Sea salt to taste	
Freshly ground pepper to taste	
Soya sauce	45ml/3 tbsp
Sherry	100ml/4fl oz
Cornflour (Cornstarch)	15ml/1 tbsp
Water	30ml/2 tbsp

For the sauce:

Butter or margarine	30g/1oz
Wholewheat flour	30g/1oz
White wine	225ml/8fl oz
Vegetable stock	225ml/8fl oz
Single cream	225ml/8fl oz
Chervil, chopped	3ml/2 tbsp

Put the flour into a bowl and combine with the salt. Add the water and mix to make a smooth pastry. Cover with a moist cloth and leave for 30 minutes.

In the meantime, heat the butter or the margarine and sauté the spring onions until translucent. Add the bean sprouts, mushrooms and chives. Season with salt,

pepper, soya sauce and sherry. Mix the cornflour with water. Stir into the vegetables until slightly thickened.

Roll out the pastry very thinly, and cut into squares. Cover each square with a little stuffing, then roll up to make

crescent shapes. Cook in salted water or deep fry in hot oil.

To make the sauce, heat the butter or margarine and stir in the flour. Pour in the wine, then add the stock and cream and stir until the sauce is smooth. Season with salt, pepper and chervil.

Spoon the sauce on to individual dishes, place the crescents on top and serve.

Spaghetti Pancakes Filled with Vegetables

Ingredients   Metric/Imperial

Wholewheat spaghetti	150g/5oz
Eggs	5/5
Sea salt to taste	
Freshly ground pepper to taste	
Nutmeg	a pinch/a pinch
Grated Parmesan cheese	50g/2oz
Oil for frying	

For the stuffing:

Ingredient	Amount
Butter or margarine	30ml/2 tbsp
Onion, chopped	1/1
Red pepper, seeded and sliced	1/1
Courgette (Zucchini), sliced	1/1
Mangetout (Snow peas)	150g/5oz
Ripe tomatoes, peeled, seeded and chopped	3/3
Vegetable stock	225ml/8fl oz
Cornflour (Cornstarch)	15–30ml/1–2 tbsp
Water	30ml/2 tbsp
Soya sauce	30ml/2 tbsp
Cider vinegar	30ml/2 tbsp
Honey	15ml/1 tbsp
Chives, snipped	30ml/2 tbsp

Cook the spaghetti in salted water until al dente, then cut into smaller lengths and place in a bowl.

Beat the eggs with salt, pepper, nutmeg and grated Parmesan. Mix with the spaghetti.

Heat a little oil in a frying pan, add a quarter of the spaghetti-egg mix on both sides, then keep warm.

Make three more pancakes from the remaining mixture.

For the stuffing, heat the butter or margarine and fry the onions until translucent. Add the pepper, courgette and mangetout. Sauté briefly. Add the tomatoes and stock, cover, then simmer over a medium heat for 5 minutes.

Combine the cornflour with cold water and add to the stuffing. Stir until the mixture thickens slightly.

Season to taste with soya sauce, vinegar, honey, salt and pepper.

Divide the vegetable stuffing on to the pancakes, fold in half and sprinkle with chives before serving.

Leek & Cheese Roly-Poly

Additionally:

Oil for greasing
Egg yolk   1/1

Pour the flour on to a large worktop. Make a well in the centre and add the eggs, oil, water and honey. Sprinkle over the salt, caraway, coriander and vinegar. Mix well and knead to make a smooth dough. Cover with a moist cloth and leave for 30 minutes.

In the meantime, to prepare the stuffing, heat the butter or margarine, add the onions and leeks and sauté until translucent. Crush the garlic with salt. Add to the pan, fry briefly, then remove the pan from the heat and leave to cool.

Beat the quark with the eggs until smooth, then fold in the vegetables and the Emmenthal. Mix with the breadcrumbs, and season with salt, pepper, chives and nutmeg.

Roll the dough out until it is approximately ¾ cm/¼ in thick. Spread a clean cloth over a pastry board or worktop and lift the pastry on to the cloth. Spread the quark mixture evenly over the pastry. Hold one side of the cloth with both hands and gently lift so that the pastry rolls over to form a loaf. Using the cloth, pat the roly-poly into a neat tubular shape. Carefully transfer to a greased baking sheet and ease away the cloth — do not allow the pastry to break. Bake for 35–40 minutes in an oven preheated to 200°C/400°F/Gas 6.

Shortly before the roly-poly is cooked, whisk the egg yolk with a little water and brush over the surface. Return to the oven to finish baking and serve warm.

Ingredients — Metric/Imperial

Ingredient	Metric/Imperial
Freshly ground wholewheat flour	200g/7oz
Egg	1/1
Oil	15ml/1 tbsp
Lukewarm water	225ml/8fl oz
Sea salt	5ml/1 tsp
Ground caraway	5ml/1 tsp
Ground coriander	2½ml/½ tsp
Honey	2½ml/½ tsp
Cider vinegar	30ml/2 tbsp

For the stuffing:

Ingredient	Metric/Imperial
Butter or margarine	50g/2oz
Onions, chopped	2/2
Leeks, sliced	2/2
Garlic cloves	2/2
Salt	5ml/1 tsp
Low-fat quark or cream cheese	225ml/8oz
Eggs	2/2
Grated Emmenthal cheese	125g/4½oz
Breadcrumbs	30–45ml/2–3 tbsp
Sea salt to taste	
Freshly ground pepper	
Nutmeg	a pinch/a pinch
Chives, snipped	30ml/2 tbsp

Lasagne Al Forno

Ingredients   Metric/Imperial

For the stuffing:

Soya granules	200g/7oz
Water	400ml/14fl oz
Low-fat quark or cream cheese	225g/8oz
Eggs, beaten	2/2
Tomato purée	30ml/2 tbsp
Butter or margarine	45ml/3 tbsp
Onion, chopped	1/1
Carrot, diced	1/1
Celeriac, diced	1/2/1/2
Wholewheat flour	30ml/2 tbsp
Tomatoes, peeled, seeded and chopped	3/3
Garlic clove, chopped	1/1
Bay leaf, crumbled	1/1
Basil, chopped	15ml/1 tbsp
Sea salt to taste	
Freshly ground pepper to taste	

For the bechamel sauce:

Butter or margarine	50g/2oz
Wholewheat flour	50g/2oz
Milk	1/2l/18fl oz
Nutmeg	a pinch/a pinch
Grated Parmesan cheese	50g/2oz

Additionally:

Green lasagne or home-made pasta	350g/12oz
Oil for greasing	
Mozzarella cheese, sliced	200g/7oz

Combine the soya granules with the water, quark, eggs and tomato purée. Leave to stand for 20 minutes.

In the meantime, heat the butter or margarine and gently fry the vegetables until translucent. Dust with flour, then add the tomatoes and bring to the boil. Add the garlic, bay leaf and basil and season with salt and pepper. Remove from the heat and combine with the soya mixture.

To make the bechamel sauce, heat the butter or margarine and stir in the flour. Add the milk, stirring constantly, then season with salt, pepper and nutmeg. Cook for 10 minutes. Add the Parmesan to the sauce.

Cook the lasagne in a tray of boiling salted water for 6 minutes.

Grease an ovenproof dish, then fill with layers of soya mixture, bechamel sauce and lasagne. Start with lasagne and end with sauce.

Cover with Mozzarella, bake for 20 minutes in an oven preheated to 200°C/400°F/Gas 6 and serve.

Tip

If you prefer, omit the soya granules and combine the quark with 100g/4oz grated Emmenthal and 30ml/2 tbsp of breadcrumbs

Boiled Potatoes with Dips

Ingredients	Metric/Imperial
New potatoes	4 large/4 large
Caraway seeds	15ml/1 tbsp
Thyme	2 sprigs/2 sprigs
Rosemary	1 sprig/1 sprig
Peppercorns	a few/a few
Juniper berries	15ml/1 tbsp
Bay leaf	1/1

Wash the potatoes thoroughly, then bring to the boil with some salted water. Add the herbs and spices, cover the pan and leave to boil, according to the size of the potatoes, for 18–20 minutes.

Remove and serve the potatoes in their skins with the dips.

Yoghurt Cheese Dip with Herbs

Ingredients	Metric/Imperial
Yoghurt	225g/8oz
Cream cheese	225 g/8 oz
Onion, chopped	1/1
Parsley, chopped	15ml/1 tbsp
Chives, snipped	15ml/1 tbsp
Lemon balm, chopped	15ml/1 tbsp
Sea salt to taste	
Freshly ground pepper to taste	
Sugar	a pinch/a pinch
Juice of lemon	1/2/1/2

Beat the yoghurt with the cream cheese until smooth. Stir in the onion and chopped herbs. Season to taste with salt, pepper, sugar and lemon juice. Serve with the boiled potatoes.

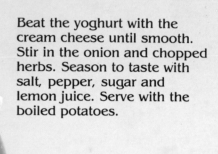

Garlic Quark Dip

Ingredients	Metric/Imperial
Low-fat quark	225g/8oz
Crème fraîche	225g/8oz
Garlic cloves	2/2
Sea salt	5ml/1 tsp
Parsley, chopped	30ml/2 tbsp
Cress	1 bunch/1 bunch
Sea salt to taste	
Freshly ground pepper to taste	
Worcester sauce	a few drops/a few drops
Lemon juice	a little/a little

Beat the quark with the crème fraîche until smooth. Crush the garlic with the salt. Stir into the quark with the herbs. Season to taste with salt, pepper, Worcester sauce and lemon juice. Serve with the boiled potatoes.

Mixed Herbs Butter

Ingredients	Metric/Imperial
Butter	225g/8oz
Onion, chopped	1/1
Parsley, chopped	30ml/2 tbsp
Thyme, chopped	30ml/2 tbsp
Oregano, chopped	30ml/2 tbsp
Tarragon, chopped	30ml/2 tbsp
Mustard	30ml/2 tbsp
Worcester sauce	a few drops/a few drops
Lemon juice	15ml/1 tbsp
Sea salt to taste	
Freshly ground pepper to taste	

Whisk the butter in a bowl until creamy. Stir the onion, herbs and mustard in to the butter.

Season to taste with Worcester sauce, lemon juice, salt and pepper. Serve with the boiled potatoes.

Blue Cheese Dip

Ingredients	Metric/Imperial
Blue cheese	100g/4oz
Butter or margarine	50g/2oz
Cream cheese	100g/4oz
Crème fraîche	100g/4oz
Onion, chopped	1/1
Parsley, chopped	30ml/2 tbsp
Chervil, chopped	30ml/2 tbsp
Sea salt to taste	
Freshly ground pepper to taste	
Sugar	a pinch/a pinch
Brandy	50ml/2fl oz
Worcester sauce	a few drops/a few drops

Cream the blue cheese with a fork. Place in to a bowl then stir in the softened butter, cream cheese and crème fraîche. Beat until smooth. Fold in the onion and herbs. Season to taste with salt, pepper and sugar, adding some brandy and Worcester sauce. Serve with the boiled potatoes.

Baked Potatoes in Soured Cream Gratin

Ingredients	Metric/Imperial
Potatoes	8 medium
Vegetable stock	300ml/10 fl oz
Sea salt to taste	
Freshly ground pepper to taste	
Ground caraway	5ml/1 tsp
Onions, chopped	2/2
Spring onions(scallions), sliced	100g/4oz

Additionally:

Soured cream	450ml/3/4 pt
Eggs, beaten	2/2
Grated Emmenthal cheese	125g/4 1/2oz
Tomatoes, peeled, seeded and sliced	4/4
Chives, snipped	30ml/2 tbsp
Flaked butter	

Slice the peeled potatoes 1 cm (½ in) thin and place in a shallow oven-proof dish. Pour over the stock, then season with salt, pepper and caraway. Sprinkle with onions and spring onions. Bake for 15 minutes in an oven pre-heated to 200°C/400°F/Gas 6.

In the meantime, combine the soured cream, eggs and Emmenthal. Spread the tomatoes over the potatoes and cover with the cream.

Place butter flakes on top, sprinkle with chives, bake for a further 10 minutes and serve.

Tip

Prepare the potatoes in small dishes to make individual servings.

Baked Potato and Kohlrabi Mornay

Ingredients	Metric/Imperial
Potatoes	4 medium/4 medium
Kohlrabi	2 medium/2 medium
Vegetable stock	100ml/4fl oz
White wine	100ml/4fl oz
Sea salt to taste	
Freshly ground pepper to taste	

For the sauce:

Butter or margarine	40g/1½oz
Wholewheat flour	40g/1½oz
Milk	300ml/10fl oz
Single cream (Light cream)	300ml/10fl oz
Nutmeg	a pinch/a pinch
Parsley, chopped	15ml/1 tbsp
Chives, snipped	15ml/1 tbsp
Mozzarella cheese, sliced	100g/4oz

Peel the potatoes and kohlrabi, then cut them into thin strips. Spread in an oven-proof dish and pour the stock and the wine on top. Sprinkle with salt and pepper. Bake for 30 minutes in an oven preheated to 200°C/400°F/Gas 6.

In the meantime, melt the butter or margarine and stir in the flour. Pour in the milk and cream and simmer gently on a low heat for 10 minutes. Stir from time to time to prevent burning. Season the sauce with salt, pepper and nutmeg. Fold in the herbs and spread over the potatoes.

Cover with Mozzarella and brown under the grill. Serve immediately.

Potato Fritters Aix-la-Chapel

Ingredients	Metric/Imperial
Potatoes	8–10 medium/8–10 medium
Wholewheat flour	225g/8oz
Egg, beaten	1/1
Sea salt to taste	
Freshly ground pepper to taste	
Nutmeg	a pinch/a pinch
Oil for frying	

For the cabbage:

Butter	60ml/4 tbsp
Onion, chopped	1/1
White cabbage, grated	1 small/1 small
White wine	225ml/8fl oz
Vegetable stock	225ml/8fl oz
Caraway seeds	5ml/1 tsp
Cider vinegar	15–30ml/1–2 tbsp
Sugar	a pinch/a pinch
Chives, snipped	30ml/2 tbsp

Boil and peel the potatoes, then press through a sieve. Add the sieved flour and egg. Season with salt, pepper and nutmeg. Mix to make a smooth pastry. Roll into fritters 2½cm (1in) thick, and fry in hot oil until brown.

To make the cabbage, heat the butter and sauté the chopped onion until translucent. Add the grated cabbage and sauté briefly. Pour in the wine and stock, and season with caraway, vinegar and sugar. Simmer over a medium heat, covered, for 25–30 minutes.

Arrange the fritters with the cabbage on a plate and sprinkle with chives.

Rice and Grains

Rice and grains have been the staple diet of every agricultural country in the world since Biblical times when the pastoral tribes fed corn and wheat to their cattle. Today they are still the main source of food in the Third World countries.

Herbed Vegetable Rice

Ingredients Metric/Imperial

Butter	50g/2oz
Onion	1/1
Broccoli florets	200g/7oz
Cauliflower florets	200g/7oz
Carrots	2/2
Leeks	1 small/1 small
White wine	225 ml/8 fl oz
Brown rice	250g/9oz
Vegetable stock	1l/1¾pt
Sea salt	
Freshly ground pepper	

Additionally:

Lemon rind	1 tbsp/1 tbsp
Lemon balm	1 sprig
Garlic cloves	2/2
Sea salt	1 tsp/1 tsp
Almond flakes	4 tbsp/4 tbsp
Eggs	4/4
Chopped sorrel, chervil, tarragon and parsley	2 tbsp each/2 tbsp each

Heat the butter in a paella pan and gently sauté the chopped onion and the broccoli and cauliflower florets in it. Peel the carrots, then slice thinly with the leeks. Add to the vegetables, pour in the wine, add the rice and cover with the stock.

Season with salt and pepper, cover and bake in the oven, heated to 200°C/400°F/Gas 6, for 20–25 minutes. Sprinkle with the lemon rind, the chopped lemon balm, the garlic crushed with salt and the almond flakes. Pour the beaten eggs on top and sprinkle with the herbs. Return to the oven and bake for a further 10 minutes, then serve immediately.

Cabbage and Rice Roulade

Ingredients Metric/Imperial

Savoy cabbage	1 small/1 small

For the stuffing:

Butter or margarine	30ml/2 tbsp
Onion, chopped	1/1
Spring onions (Scallions), sliced	100g/4oz
Raisins	30ml/2 tbsp
Flaked almonds	60ml/4tbsp
Boiled brown rice	250g/9oz
Eggs, beaten	2/2
Mozzarella cheese, diced	200g/7oz
Chives, snipped	30 ml/2 tbsp

For the Sauce:

Tomatoes, peeled, seeded and chopped	500g/1lb
Onion, chopped	1 small/1 small
Garlic clove, chopped	1/1
Butter	15 ml/1 tbsp
Freshly ground pepper to taste	

Basil, chopped   15ml/1 tbsp
Grated Gouda or
Cheddar cheese 100g/4oz

Carefully separate the cabbage leaves and parboil them for 5 minutes in salted water. Remove the rib from each leaf. Drain well and spread out on a worktop.

For the stuffing, heat the butter or margarine in a pan and sauté the onion and spring onions until translucent. Stir in the raisins, almonds and rice. Remove the pan from the heat and leave to cool.

Fold the eggs, Mozzarella and chives into the rice.

Spread the stuffing equally on the cabbage leaves, then roll them up to make roulades. Place in a single layer in an oven-proof dish.

Sauté the onion and garlic in butter until translucent. Add the tomatoes, salt and pepper. Cook for 10 minutes.

Pour the sauce through a sieve, season with basil and pour over the cabbage roulades.

Sprinkle with Gouda or Cheddar and bake in an oven

preheated to 200°C/400°F/Gas 6 for 35–40 minutes.

81

Savoury Choux Fritters

Ingredients Metric/Imperial

Vegetable stock	250ml/9fl oz
Butter or margarine	50g/2oz
Sea salt to taste	
Freshly ground pepper to taste	
Nutmeg	a pinch/a pinch
Freshly ground wheat flour	140g/5oz
Cornflour (Cornstarch)	40g/1 1/2oz
Wheatgerm	100g/4oz
Eggs, beaten	4–5/4–5
Parmesan cheese	125g/4 1/2oz
Chives, snipped	30ml/2 tbsp
Oil for deep frying	

Place the stock and the butter or margarine in a pan and bring to the boil. Season with salt, pepper and nutmeg. Stir in the flour, wheat and cornflour. Continue stirring until the mixture comes off the bottom of the pan like a choux pastry.

Add the eggs a little bit at a time and then the cheese, wheatgerm and chives.

Drop spoonsful of the mixture, one at a time, into hot fat. Be sure to dip the spoon into the fat between each addition to make handling easier. When the fritters are golden, drain well. Serve either warm or cold.

Tip

Serve the fritters with herbed cream cheese and a fresh salad.

Barley Cake Garni

Ingredients	Metric/Imperial
Butter or margarine	50g/2oz
Onion, chopped	1/1
Red pepper, seeded and diced	1/1
Barley	200g/7oz
Vegetable stock	½ l/18fl oz
White wine	225ml/8fl oz
Garlic cloves	2/2
Sea salt to taste	
Freshly ground pepper to taste	
Bechamel sauce	450ml/16fl oz
Grated Emmenthal cheese	225ml/8fl oz
Breadcrumbs	
Chives, snipped	30ml/2tbsp
Parsley, chopped	30 ml/2 tbsp
Nutmeg	a pinch/a pinch
Egg yolks	3/3
Egg whites	3/3
Oil for greasing	

Additionally:

Boiled potato, sliced	1 medium/ 1 medium
Tomatoes, peeled, seeded and sliced	2/2
Cucumber, sliced	½ small/½ small
Radishes, sliced	4–5/4–5
Sprigs of herbs	
Stock	250ml/9fl oz
Gelatine powder	25g/1oz

Heat the butter or margarine and gently fry the vegetables until translucent. Add the washed barley and sauté briefly. Pour in the wine and stock.

Crush the garlic cloves with salt. Add to the stock, season with salt and pepper, cover and leave to simmer over a medium heat for 40 minutes.

Uncover the pan and cook over a high heat until all the liquid has evaporated. Remove from the heat and cool.

Fold in the bechamel sauce and the cheese. If necessary, bind with breadcrumbs.

Add the herbs, then season with salt, pepper and nutmeg.

Stir the egg yolks into the mixture, then carefully fold in the stiffly beaten egg whites.

Grease a round baking tray, sprinkle with breadcrumbs, then transfer the barley mixture into it.

Bake in an oven preheated to 200°C/400°F/Gas 6 for 40 minutes. Cool completely.

Arrange the potato and tomatoes on the cake. Decorate with herbs, cucumber and radishes.

Dissolve the gelatine in stock and pour over the vegetables on the cake. Leave

to cool in the fridge, then cut into slices and garnish with mayonnaise before serving.

Tip

Strict vegetarians can replace the gelatine with agar-agar which is made from algae. (Use 2 teaspoons per 600 ml/1 pint of water, boiled for 8 minutes.)

Oat Cutlet Milanese

Ingredients   Metric/Imperial

Butter or margarine	30ml/2 tbsp
Onion, chopped	1/1
Leek, sliced	1 small/1 small
Vegetable stock	½ l/18fl oz
Sea salt	5ml/1 tsp
Thyme, chopped	5ml/1 tsp
Marjoram, chopped	15ml/1 tbsp
Rolled oats	160g/5½oz

Additionally:

Eggs, beaten	3/3
Mustard	30ml/2 tbsp
Green peppercorns	5ml/1 tsp
Chives, snipped	30 ml/2 tbsp
Breadcrumbs for binding	30–45ml/ 2–3 tbsp
Olive oil for frying	

For the sauce:

Butter or margarine	30ml/2 tbsp
Onion, chopped	1/1
Red pepper, seeded and chopped	1/1
Sweetcorn (Corn kernels)	100g/4oz
Tomato ketchup	100ml/4fl oz
Vegetable stock	225ml/8fl oz
Crème fraîche	100g/4oz
Curry powder	5ml/1 tsp
Paprika	5ml/1 tsp
Tabasco (Hot pepper sauce)	a few drops/ a few drops
Sugar	a pinch/a pinch

Heat the butter or margarine and sauté the vegetables until translucent. Pour in the stock, season with salt, thyme and marjoram and stir in the oats. Cover and simmer over a medium heat for 30 minutes.

Remove from the heat, cool, then stir in the eggs, mustard, peppercorns and chives. Bind with breadcrumbs, then shape into

cutlets. Shallow fry in olive oil until golden brown, then transfer to a serving dish and keep warm.

To make the sauce, heat the butter or margarine and sauté the onion and pepper until translucent. Add the drained sweetcorn, then the

ketchup and stock. Stir in the crème fraîche, curry powder, paprika, Tabasco or pepper sauce, salt, pepper and sugar.

Arrange the cutlets on a plate, spoon over the sauce and serve.

Buckwheat Pancakes with Cherries and Butterscotch Sauce

Ingredients Metric/Imperial

Buckwheat flour	100g/4oz
Eggs	3/3
Sea salt	a pinch/a pinch
Milk	250ml/9fl oz
Sugar	10ml/2 tsp
Oil for frying	50ml/2fl oz

Additionally:

Butter or margarine	15–30ml/2 tbsp
Sugar	45ml/3 tbsp
Green peppercorns	15ml/1 tbsp
Red wine	450ml/16fl oz
Cherries, stoned (pitted)	200g/7oz
Ground cloves	a pinch/a pinch
Ground cinnamon	2½ ml/½ tsp
Cornflour (Cornstarch)	5ml/1 tsp
Water	75ml/5 tbsp

Beat the eggs and add the flour, salt, milk and sugar to make a smooth batter.

Heat the oil in a frying pan and pour in some batter. Cook until set, toss and cook on the second side. Keep warm on plates or a tray.

Heat the butter or margarine in a pan with the sugar until the sauce is smooth and bubbly like a butterscotch syrup, approximately 4 minutes.

Boil the stoned cherries with the wine and sugar for 2 minutes. Thicken with the combined cornflour and water. The sauce should begin to clear. Flavour with cinnamon, cloves and a few green peppercorns if you like.

Millet Cakes with Pineapple Sauerkraut

Ingredients

	Metric/Imperial
Millet	150g/5oz
Vegetable stock	½l/18fl oz
Olive oil	10ml/2tsp
Onions, chopped	2/2
Sea salt to taste	
Freshly ground white pepper to taste	
Marjoram, chopped	15ml/1 tbsp
Chives, snipped	30ml/2 tbsp
Eggs, beaten	2/2
Oats for binding	30–60 ml/ 2–4 tbsp

Additionally:

Wholewheat breadcrumbs	45–60ml/ 3–4 tbsp
Oil for frying	

For the pineapple sauerkraut:

Butter or margarine	30ml/2 tbsp
Onion, chopped	1/1
Pineapple	4 slices/4 slices
Sauerkraut	500g/1lb
Vegetable stock	500ml/1pt
Green peppercorns	5ml/1 tsp
Honey	30ml/2 tbsp
Cress	1 box/1 box

Wash the millet, add to the boiling stock and simmer over a medium heat for 20 minutes.

Fry the onion in oil until golden brown and add to the millet. Season with salt, pepper and marjoram. Cool then add the chives and eggs. Bind with oats.

Using wet hands, shape little cakes out of the mixture.

Turn in the wholewheat breadcrumbs and shallow fry in hot oil until golden brown. Drain and keep warm.

To make the pineapple sauerkraut, heat the butter or margarine and gently soften the onion. Add the finely diced pineapple and the

sauerkraut, then pour in the stock. Season with salt, pepper and green peppercorns. Simmer, covered, for 30 minutes.

Adjust the seasoning then add the honey and finally the cress.

Arrange the millet cakes, on plates, spread sauerkraut on top and serve.

Millet Loaf Hamburg-Style

Ingredients	Metric/Imperial
Butter or margarine	30ml/2 tbsp
Onion, chopped	1/1
Leek, sliced	1/1
Red pepper, seeded and diced	1/1
Carrots, diced	2/2
Blanched peas	100g/4oz
Millet	200g/7oz
Vegetable stock	½l/18 fl oz
Parsley, chopped	30ml/2 tbsp
Lemon balm, chopped	15ml/1 tbsp
Dandelion leaves	12/12
Eggs, beaten	2/2
Grated Gouda or Cheddar cheese	100g/4oz
Sea salt to taste	
Freshly ground black pepper to taste	

Additionally:

Oil for greasing	
Mozzarella cheese, sliced	100g/4oz

Heat the butter or margarine and sauté the onion. Add the other vegetables and fry briefly. Stir in the washed millet, pour in the stock, cover and simmer for 20 minutes.

Remove from the heat, then stir in the herbs, eggs and cheese. Season with salt and pepper. Transfer to a greased ovenproof dish.

Cover with Mozzarella and bake for 15–20 minutes in an oven preheated to 200°C/400°F/Gas 6.

Salads

Vegetarian cooking without salads is like a soup without salt! Combined with pasta or grains, they make a light lunch or supper. The many vegetable variations can also constitute a wonderful, light starter to a vegetarian dinner while simultaneously providing essential vitamins and minerals.

Pineapple Sauerkraut Salad

Ingredients   Metric/Imperial

Ingredient	Metric/Imperial
Sauerkraut	400g/14oz
Pineapple, fresh or tinned	4 slices/4 slices
Tomatoes, peeled, seeded and chopped	4/4
Cress	1 box/1 box
Low-fat yoghurt	450g/16oz
Orange	1/1
Sea salt to taste	
Freshly ground pepper to taste	
Worcester sauce	15ml/1 tbsp

Break up the sauerkraut with a fork and place in a bowl with the diced pineapple.

Add the tomatoes and cress to the sauerkraut.

Combine the yoghurt with the orange juice. Season to taste with salt, pepper and Worcester sauce. Pour over the sauerkraut, mix well and transfer to four individual bowls.

Celeriac Salad

Ingredients   Metric/Imperial

Ingredient	Metric/Imperial
Celeriac	2/2
Apples, not too sweet	2/2
Grated walnuts	100g/4oz
Lemon	1/1
Yoghurt	225g/8oz
Crème fraîche	225g/8oz
Sea salt to taste	
Freshly ground pepper to taste	
Sugar	a pinch/a pinch
Mustard	5ml/1 tsp
Chives, snipped	30ml/2 tbsp

Tip

If you find the raw celeriac too strong in flavour, you can parboil it and then finely dice.

Peel and coarsely grate the celeriac.

Peel, core and coarsely grate the apples. Mix with the celeriac. Fold in the walnuts and lemon juice.

Combine the yoghurt with the crème fraîche, salt, pepper, sugar and mustard and dress the salad with this mixture.

Arrange in individual bowls, sprinkle with chives and serve.

Beetroot and Tangerine Salad

Ingredients	Metric/Imperial
Beetroot (Beet)	400g/14oz
Tangerines	2/2
Spring onions (Scallions), sliced	100g/4oz
Lemon	1/1
Ground nut oil	15ml/1 tbsp
Sea salt to taste	
Freshly ground pepper to taste	
Soured cream	225g/8oz
Cress	1 box/1 box

Finely slice or coarsely grate the beetroot.

Peel the tangerines, separate into segments and mix with the spring onions and beetroot. Season with lemon juice, oil, salt and pepper.

Divide into four individual bowls and garnish with cream and cress before serving.

. . . .

Tip

For a spicy variation on this theme, add 2 1/2ml/1/2 tsp grated horseradish to the dressing.

. . . .

Carrot and Orange Salad

Ingredients	Metric/Imperial
Carrots	8 medium/8 medium
Oranges	2/2
Chopped walnuts	100g/4oz
Chervil, snipped	30g/2 tbsp
Sea salt to taste	
Freshly ground pepper to taste	
Lemon	1/1
Nut oil	15ml/1 tbsp

Peel the carrots and grate them coarsely into a bowl.

Peel the oranges and separate them into segments. Dice and add to the carrots along with the chervil and walnuts. Dress with salt, pepper, lemon juice and oil.

Arrange the salad in champagne glasses and serve.

Potato Salad with Herbed Garlic Sauce

Tip

If you find the taste of garlic too strong, simply rub your salad bowl with half a clove instead of adding whole cloves to the salad or replace with finely chopped shallots.

Ingredients

Ingredients	Metric/Imperial
Potatoes	3–4 large/3–4 large
Caraway seeds	15ml/1 tbsp
Thyme	a sprig/a sprig
Rosemary	a sprig/a sprig

For the dressing:

Onions, chopped	2/2
Spring onions (Scallions), sliced	100g/4oz
Low-fat quark	100g/4oz
Yoghurt	225g/8oz
Crème fraîche	225g/8oz
Lemon	1/1
Cider vinegar	45ml/3 tbsp
Sea salt	15ml/1 tbsp
Garlic cloves	6/6
Freshly ground white pepper	
Sugar (optional)	5ml/1 tsp
Chives, snipped	30ml/2 tbsp
Parsley, chopped	15ml/1 tbsp
Tarragon, chopped	15ml/1 tbsp
Capers (pickled)	15ml/1 tbsp

Cover the potatoes with salted water. Add the caraway seeds, thyme and rosemary. Cover and boil for 20 minutes.

Combine the quark with the yoghurt, crème fraîche, lemon juice and vinegar. Mix with the onions and spring onions. Crush the garlic with salt and add then season with pepper and sugar.

Add the herbs and drained capers. Adjust the seasoning.

Peel and slice the potatoes, then transfer to a bowl.

Cool then dress with the garlic sauce and marinate for at least 30 minutes. Adjust seasoning and serve.

Madrid Salad

Ingredients

Ingredients	Metric/Imp
Hard-boiled eggs (Hard-cooked eggs)	8/8
Radicchio	1 small/1 s
Iceberg lettuce	1 small/1 s
Large tomatoes	2/2
Black olives	100g/4oz
Capers (pickled)	30ml/2 tbs
Goat's cheese	150g/5oz
Feta cheese	150g/5oz
Spanish onion	1/1

For the dressing:

Olive oil	100ml/4 floz
Red wine vinegar	100ml/4floz
Oregano, chopped	15ml/1 tbsp
Lemon balm, chopped	15ml/1 tbsp
Chives, snipped	15ml/1 tbsp
Mint, chopped	15ml/1 tbsp
Salt to taste	
Freshly ground pepper to taste	

Shell the eggs, cut them into eight wedges and place in a bowl.

Tear the washed radicchio and iceberg lettuce into bite-size pieces.

Finely dice the tomatoes. Add the olives and the

drained capers to the salad.

Flake the goat's cheese and the Feta with a fork and slice the onion.

Gently mix all the ingredients with the eggs.

Combine the oil, vinegar and herbs. Season with salt

and pepper. Dress the salad and serve.

Sweet and Savoury

Have a try at vegetarian baking! Using wholewheat flour and honey might seem somewhat unusual in the beginning, but you'll soon discover how well they go with many fruits and vegetables.

Mushroom Doughnuts

Ingredients

Ingredients	Metric/Imperial
Butter or margarine	50g/2oz
Vegetable stock	300ml/10fl oz
Sea salt	a pinch/a pinch
Wholewheat flour	150g/5oz
Eggs, beaten	4/4
Baking powder	2½ml/½ tsp
Frying oil	

For the stuffing:

Butter	15ml/1 tbsp
Mushrooms, sliced	250g/9oz
Herbed cream cheese (Boursin)	200g/7oz
White wine	100ml/4fl oz
Parsley, chopped	15ml/1 tbsp
Tomatoes, skinned, seeded and chopped	2/2
Green peppercorns in brine	15ml/1 tbsp
Sea salt to taste	
Freshly ground pepper to taste	
Caraway seeds	a pinch/a pinch
Worcester sauce	5ml/1 tsp

Put the butter, stock and salt in a pan and bring to the boil. Add the flour and stir until the mixture comes off the bottom of the pan. Remove from the heat.

Add the eggs, a little at a time, then fold in the baking powder.

Using two teaspoons, make little doughnuts from the pastry.

Deep-fry in hot oil until golden brown, then remove and keep warm.

To make the stuffing, heat the butter and sauté the mushrooms. Cool slightly, then stir in the cream cheese and the wine. Fold in the parsley, tomatoes and drained peppercorns.

Season to taste with salt, pepper, caraway seeds and Worcester sauce.

Halve the doughnuts and fill with the cheese mixture. Replace the lids and serve.

Feta Pie with Herbs

Ingredients

	Metric/Imperial
Phyllo pastry,	450g/1lb
Butter or margarine	40g/1½oz
Flour	40g/1½oz
White wine	225ml/8fl oz
Milk	300ml/10fl oz
Feta cheese	450g/1lb
Eggs, beaten	6/6
Chives, snipped	30ml/2 tbsp
Parsley, chopped	30ml/2 tbsp
Garlic cloves	2/2
Sea salt to taste	
Freshly ground pepper to taste	
Nutmeg	a pinch/a pinch
Oil for greasing	
Egg yolks	2/2
Coriander seeds, crushed	15ml/1 tbsp
Caraway seeds, crushed	15ml/1 tbsp
Cardamom pods, crushed	15ml/1 tbsp

Heat the butter or margarine and mix in the flour. Add the wine and milk, stirring constantly. Bring the sauce to the boil then remove from the heat and crumble in the Feta.

Gently fold in the eggs and herbs.

Crush the garlic with salt and add to the cheese mixture. Season to taste with salt, pepper and nutmeg.

Gently place a sheet of phyllo pastry in the base of a greased, round baking tin. Spread with some of the cheese sauce. Continue alternating layers of pastry and sauce, ending with a layer of pastry.

Combine the egg yolks with a little water and brush over the top layer of pastry. Sprinkle with crushed coriander, caraway and cardamom.

Bake the pie for 30 minutes in an oven preheated to 200°C/400°F/Gas 6. Remove and serve.

Fruit Pizza

Ingredients   Metric/Imperial

For the pastry:

Wholewheat flour	400g/14oz
Dried yeast	10g/1 tsp
Vanilla essence	6 drops/6 drops
Grated orange rind	15ml/1 tbsp
Sea salt	a pinch/a pinch
Lukewarm water	225ml/8fl oz
Oil	30ml/2 tbsp

For the topping:

Pineapple	4 slices/4 slices
Peach halves	4/4
Bananas	4/4
Kiwi fruit (Chinese gooseberries)	4/4
Black cherries (fresh or tinned)	100g/4oz

Additionally:

Low-fat quark	225g/8oz
Single cream (Light cream)	225ml/8fl oz
Eggs	4/4
Vanilla essence	6/6
Castor sugar	30ml/2 tbsp
Orange liqueur	50ml/2fl oz

Combine the yeast with 5ml/1 tsp flour and 45ml/3 tbsp tepid water. Leave for 10 minutes to activate.

Combine the flour with the yeast mixture, vanilla essence,

orange rind and the salt. Pour in the oil and water and mix to make a smooth dough.

Cover with a moist tea towel and leave to rise for 30 minutes. Roll out thinly and transfer to four pizza tins.

Cut the pineapple, peaches, peeled bananas and the kiwi fruit into small pieces and spread on the pizzas. Spread the cherries on top.

Combine the quark with the cream and eggs, then add the vanilla essence and sugar. Flavour with liqueur, then spread the quark mixture equally on pizzas.

Bake in an oven preheated to 200°C/400°F/Gas 6 for 20–25 minutes. Serve immediately.

Vegetable Pizza Romana

Ingredients — Metric/Imperial

Ingredient	Metric/Imperial
Strong white flour	200g/7oz
Wholewheat flour	200g/7oz
Dried yeast	10g/1 tsp
Sugar	15ml/1 tbsp
Lukewarm water	300ml/10 fl oz
Sea salt	5ml/1 tsp
Olive oil	30ml/2 tbsp

For the topping:

Ingredient	Metric/Imperial
Tomato purée	60ml/4 tbsp
Courgette (Zucchini), sliced	1 small/1 small
Spanish onion, sliced	1/1
Red pepper, seeded and sliced	1/1
Mushrooms sliced	100g/4oz
Tomatoes, peeled, seeded and sliced	4/4
Sea salt to taste	
Freshly ground pepper to taste	
Oregano, chopped	30ml/2 tbsp
Chives, snipped	30ml/2 tbsp
Mozzarella cheese, sliced	200g/7oz

Combine the yeast with 5ml/ 1 tsp flour and 45ml/3 tbsp tepid water. Leave for 10 minutes to activate.

Combine the flour with the yeast mixture and the sugar. Pour in the warm water, then add the salt and oil. Knead to make a smooth dough. Cover with a moist cloth and leave to rise in a warm place for 30–45 minutes.

Knead well, then roll out thinly and cover the base of four small pizza tins with the pastry.

Cover each base with 15ml/1 tbsp of tomato purée and top with courgette, onion, pepper, mushrooms and tomato slices. Sprinkle with salt, pepper, oregano and chives.

Cover with Mozzarella and transfer to an oven preheated to 200°C/400°F/Gas 6. Bake for about 20 minutes, then remove and serve.

Quiche Lorraine

Ingredients   Metric/Imperial

Wholewheat flour	300g/11oz
Butter or margarine	175g/6oz
Egg yolks	2/2
Water	75ml/5 tbsp
Sea salt	5ml/1 tsp

For the topping:

Butter or margarine	30ml/2 tbsp
Spanish onions, sliced	2/2
Leeks, sliced	2/2
Sea salt to taste	
Freshly ground pepper to taste	
Nutmeg	a pinch/a pinch
Ground caraway	2½ml/½ tsp
Single cream (light cream)	225ml/8fl oz
Eggs	4/4
Chives, snipped	30ml/2 tbsp
Parsley, chopped	30ml/2 tbsp

Put the flour on a worktop, then flake the butter or margarine on top. Add the yolks, water and salt and quickly combine to make a smooth dough. Roll into a

ball and wrap in polythene or clingfilm. Leave for at least 1 hour in the fridge.

To make the topping, heat the butter or margarine and gently fry the onions and leeks until translucent. Season with salt, pepper, nutmeg and caraway.

Roll out the dough thinly and cover the base of a baking tray or tin. Prick the base all over with a fork, then spread the vegetables on top.

Beat the cream with the eggs, salt, pepper and herbs.

Pour over the vegetables and bake for 30 minutes in an oven preheated to 200°C/400°F/Gas 6.

Remove and serve either warm or cold.

Country Spicy Flat Bread

Ingredients Metric/Imperial

Strong white flour	350g/12oz
Wholewheat flour	150g/5oz
Dried yeast	10g/1 tsp
Sea salt	5ml/1 tsp
Honey	15ml/1 tbsp
Milk	125ml/4fl oz
Water	125ml/4fl oz
Butter or margarine	50g/2oz
Caraway seeds	5ml/1 tsp
Coriander	5ml/1 tsp
Cardamom	5ml/1 tsp

Additionally:

Milk	60ml/4 tbsp
Sesame seeds	60ml/4 tbsp
Oil for greasing	

Combine the yeast with 5ml/1 tsp flour and 45ml/3 tbsp tepid water. Leave for 10 minutes to activate.

Mix the flour with the yeast mixture, salt and honey in a bowl. Add the milk, water butter or margarine and spices. Combine to make a smooth dough. Cover and leave to rise in a warm place for about 30–45 minutes.

Knead well, then shape into little flat cakes. Place on a greased baking tray. Brush with milk and sprinkle with the sesame seeds. Cover and leave to rise for 15 minutes.

Bake for 25–30 minutes in an oven preheated to 200°C/400°F/Gas 6. Remove and serve either slightly warm or cold.

Herb Rolls

Ingredients Metric/Imperial

Freshly ground wholewheat flour	500g/1lb
Dried yeast	10g/1 tsp
Sea salt	5ml/1 tsp
Sugar	15ml/1 tbsp
Milk	225ml/8 fl oz
Butter or margarine	50g/2 oz
Egg yolks	2/2
Marjoram, chopped	15ml/1 tbsp
Thyme, chopped	5ml/1 tsp
Parsley, chopped	15ml/1 tbsp
Chives, snipped	15ml/1 tbsp

Additionally:

Egg yolks	2/2
Caraway seeds	15ml/1 tbsp
Coriander seeds	15ml/1 tbsp

Combine the yeast with 5ml/
1 tsp flour and 45ml/3 tbsp
tepid water. Leave for
10 minutes to activate.

Combine the flour with the
yeast mixture, salt and sugar.
Add the lukewarm milk,
butter and egg yolks. Add the
marjoram, thyme, parsley
and chives. Mix to make a
smooth pastry. Cover and
leave to rise in a warm place
for 30–45 minutes.

Knead thoroughly, then roll
out on a floured worktop to
about 2–3cm (¾–1¼ in) in
thickness.

Using a round shape, cut
out little rolls. Place on a
floured baking tray, cover and
leave to rise for a further
15 minutes.

Brush with egg yolk
combined with water and
sprinkle with caraway and
coriander seeds.

Bake for 15 minutes in an
oven preheated to
200°C/400°F/Gas 6 and serve
warm or cold.

Buttermilk Bread

Ingredients	Metric/Imperial
Freshly ground spelt	675g/1lb 7oz
Dried yeast	10g/1 tsp
Buttermilk	½ l/18fl oz
Honey	30ml/2 tbsp
Sea salt	5ml/1 tsp
Ground caraway	5ml/1 tsp
Ground coriander	5ml/1 tsp
Allspice	a pinch/a pinch
Oil for greasing	

Combine the yeast with 5ml/
1 tsp spelt and 45ml/3 tbsp
tepid water. Leave to activate
for 10 minutes.

Combine the spelt with the
yeast mixture. Add the
buttermilk and honey. Mix to
make a smooth dough.
Season with salt, caraway,
coriander and allspice.

Place the dough in a
greased loaf pan. Cover and
leave to rise in a warm place
for 30–45 minutes.

Bake for 45–50 minutes in
an oven preheated to
200°C/400°F/Gas 6. Remove,
leave to cool completely and
serve.

Tip

*Spelt, also called German
wheat, is a special kind of
wheat. You can replace it
with other wheat.*

Sweet Corncake with Strawberry Butter

Ingredients	Metric/Imperial
Wholewheat flour	150g/5oz
Cornmeal (maize)	150g/5oz
Baking powder	10ml/2 tsp
Sea salt	a pinch/a pinch
Yoghurt	225g/8oz
Honey	50g/2oz
Eggs	2/2
Oil	60ml/4 tbsp

For the butter:

Strawberries	250g/9oz
Lemon	1/1
Butter	150g/5oz
Vanilla essence	6 drops/6 drops
Castor sugar (superfine sugar)	30ml/2 tbsp

Combine the flour, cornmeal, baking powder and salt in a mixing bowl. Add the yoghurt, honey, eggs and oil. Mix to make a smooth dough. Turn on to a floured worktop and roll out until the dough is approximately 1¼ cm/½ inch thick. Cut into rounds approximately 6 cm/2½ inches in diameter. Place the corncakes on a greased baking tray and bake for 10–15 minutes in an oven preheated to 200°C/400°F/ Gas 6.

In the meantime, purée the strawberries.

Add the lemon juice and vanilla essence to the butter and whisk until creamy.

Add the strawberry purée and sugar to the butter. Combine well with a whisk, then leave to cool in the fridge.

Serve the corncakes with the strawberry butter.

Sweetcorn Balls

Ingredients	Metric/Imperial
Eggs	2/2
Honey	50g/2oz
Wholewheat flour	50g/2oz
Ground almonds	50g/2oz
Sweetcorn (Corn kernels)	250g/9oz
Oil for deep-frying	

For the sauce:

Demerara sugar	50g/2oz
Butter	30ml/2 tbsp
Red wine	500ml/18fl oz
Morello cherries, stoned	250g/9oz
Cinnamon	2½ml/½ tsp
Vanilla essence	6 drops/6 drops
Icing sugar (Confectioners' sugar)	5ml/1 tsp

Whisk the eggs with the honey until creamy. Fold in the flour and almonds. Stir in the drained sweetcorn.

Using two teaspoons, cut off little balls from the mixture and deep-fry in hot

oil until golden brown. Remove and keep warm.

To make the sauce, caramelize the sugar and butter in a frying pan. Pour in the wine, then add the cherries and bring to the boil once.

Season with cinnamon and vanilla essence and bind with some icing sugar.

Serve the sweetcorn balls with the sauce.

Yoghurt Torte with Fruits

Ingredients   Metric/Imperial

For the pastry:

Eggs	2/2
Honey	80–100g/3–4oz
Sieved wholewheat flour	100g/4oz
Baking powder	10ml/2 tsp
Vanilla essence	6 drops/6 drops

For the filling:

Yoghurt	500g/1lb
Whipping cream	225ml/8fl oz
Honey	75g/3oz
Vanilla essence	6 drops/6 drops
Gelatine	25g/1oz
Castor (Superfine) sugar	25g/1oz

For decorating:

Fruit, according to season	*100g/4oz*
Melted jam	*50g/2oz*
Flaked almonds	*100g/4oz*

Whisk the eggs with the honey until fluffy. Combine the flour with the baking powder. Add to the eggs along with the vanilla essence. Make into a smooth pastry, roll out, and transfer to a greased round baking tin. Bake for about 20 minutes in an oven preheated to 200°C/400°F/Gas 6. Remove and cool.

In the meantime, put the yoghurt in a bowl.

Whisk the cream until firm. Stir the honey and vanilla essence into the yoghurt.

Combine the gelatine and sugar. Dissolve in 100ml/4fl oz boiling water and stir into the yoghurt. Cool then carefully fold in the whipped cream. Leave to set for 5 minutes, then spread on the pastry base.

Garnish with fruit and glaze with jam. Leave to set completely in the fridge, then remove from the baking tin.

Toast the flaked almonds and garnish the edge of the gateau.

Tip

You can replace the yoghurt with buttermilk or Biogarde.

Apricot tart with coconut

Ingredients	Metric/Imperial
Egg yolks	8/8
Butter or margarine	200g/7oz
Honey	180–200g/6–7oz
Finely ground wholewheat flour	500g/1lb
Sea salt	a pinch/a pinch

For the topping:

Fresh apricots, halved	1kg/2lb
Egg whites	8/8

Castor (Superfine), sugar	200g/7oz
Desiccated coconut (Shredded coconut)	400g/14oz

Additionally:

Oil for greasing
Wholewheat breadcrumbs for sprinkling

In a bowl, whisk the egg yolks, butter and honey until creamy.

Combine the flour with the salt, add to the eggs and combine to make a smooth pastry.

Roll out and transfer to a greased baking tray sprinkled

with breadcrumbs. Cover with halved apricots. Bake for 15–20 minutes in an oven preheated to 200°C/ 400°F/Gas 6.

In the meantime, whisk the egg whites until stiff. Gradually sprinkle in the sugar, whisking constantly. Fold in the desiccated coconut. Spread the coconut mixture on the prebaked cake, then bake for a further 25–30 minutes.

Remove, cut into squares while still warm and serve.

Chocolate Cherry Slice

Ingredients	Metric/Imperial
Butter or margarine	200g/7oz
Sugar	250g/9oz
Finely ground rye flour	250g/9oz
Ground hazelnuts	250g/9oz
Eggs	4/4
Cinnamon	10ml/2 tsp
Cocoa powder	45ml/3 tbsp
Vanilla essence	several drops/ several drops
Baking powder	5ml/1 tsp
Cherry liqueur	15ml/1 tbsp
Stoned cherries (Pitted cherries)	1kg/2lb

Additionally:

Breadcrumbs for sprinkling
Oil for greasing
Icing sugar (Confectioners sugar) for dusting

Whisk the softened butter with the sugar until creamy.

Combine the flour with the baking powder and nuts.

Whisk the eggs one after the other into the butter mixture.

Alternating, fold the flour, cinnamon, cocoa powder, vanilla essence and liqueur into the eggs.

Roll out the pastry and transfer to a baking tray greased with oil and sprinkled with breadcrumbs. Spread the cherries on top. Bake for

25–30 minutes in an oven preheated to 200°C/400°F/ Gas 6.

Remove, cut into pieces while still warm, dust with icing sugar and serve.

Sweets

Fresh Fruit Muesli

Ingredients	Metric/Imperial
Mixed grains (wheat, rye, barley, oats)	120g/4¹/₂oz
Apple	1/1
Pear	1/1
Fresh strawberries	100g/4oz
Redcurrants	100g/4oz
Raisins	60ml/4 tbsp
Chopped hazelnuts	50g/2oz
Vanilla essence	6 drops/6 drops
Castor sugar (Superfine sugar)	15 ml/1 tbsp
Yoghurt	100g/4oz
Crème fraîche or soured cream	50 g/2 oz

Mix the grains with the fruit and serve immediately.

Rough-grind the grains, mix with water to make a thick porridge and leave to soak overnight.

Quarter and core the apple and pear, then slice thinly.

Wash the strawberries and currants. Drain well, then add with other fruit to the grains. Stir in the raisins and hazelnuts. Combine the vanilla essence, sugar and yoghurt with the crème fraîche or soured cream. Sweeten to taste.

Tip

You can prepare this muesli with other fruits. Soak some dried fruit with the grains and add them, chopped, to the muesli.

Muesli with Raspberry Cream

Ingredients   Metric/Imperial

Mixed grains or:	120g/4½oz
Six-grain muesli	250g/9oz

For the raspberry cream:

Milk	225ml/8fl oz
Egg yolks	4/4
Vanilla essence	6 drops/6 drops
Crème fraîche	225g/8oz
Yoghurt	500g/16oz
Honey	45–60ml/ 3–4 tbsp
Fresh raspberries	150g/5oz

Rough-grind the grains, mix with water to make a thick porridge and leave to soak overnight. (Muesli mix does

not need to be soaked.)

Combine the milk with the egg yolks and vanilla essence. Whisk in a double boiler until creamy.

Remove from the heat, then fold in the crème fraîche and yoghurt. Sweeten with honey according to taste.

Add the raspberries, then the grains or muesli, and serve.

Orange Muesli
with Chocolate Milk

Ingredients	Metric/Imperial
Oranges	2/2
Rolled oats	250g/9oz
Milk	1/2 l/18fl oz
Dark chocolate (Semi-sweet chocolate), grated	100g/4oz
Desiccated coconut (Shredded coconut)	50g/2oz
Vanilla essence	6 drops/6 drops
Honey	30–45ml/ 2–3 tbsp
Cinnamon	a pinch/a pinch

Separate the oranges into segments and remove the thin skin, then cut into small pieces. Mix the oranges with the oats.

Heat the milk and dissolve the chocolate in it. Stir in the coconut, vanilla essence, honey and cinnamon.

Arrange the muesli in a bowl, pour the chocolate milk on top and serve immediately.

115

Cornflakes with Blueberry Milk

Ingredients	Metric/Imperial
Cornflakes	200g/7oz
Butter or margarine	30ml/2 tbsp
Sugar	50g/2oz
Milk	½l/18fl oz
Custard powder (Birds' English dessert mix)	30ml/2 tbsp
Ground cinnamon	pinch/pinch
Blueberries	150g/5oz
Crème fraîche	225g/8oz
Raisins	60ml/4 tbsp
Toasted flaked almonds	60ml/4 tbsp

Divide the cornflakes into four bowls.

Heat the butter or margarine and caramelize the sugar. Add the milk and dissolve the sugar. Add the custard powder, combined with a little milk, to the pan. Add the cinnamon and bring to the boil once, stirring frequently. Fold the

blueberries and crème fraîche into the custard.

Spoon the blueberry milk over the cornflakes, sprinkle with raisins and almonds and serve.

Nutty Flakes with Fruit

Ingredients	Metric/Imperial
Cornflakes	200g/7oz
Hazelnuts	50g/2oz
Pine kernels	50g/2oz
Walnuts	50g/2oz
Unsalted peanuts	50g/2oz
Raisins	100g/4oz
Banana, diced	1/1
Apple, grated	1/1
Milk	½l/18fl oz
Honey	60ml/4 tbsp
Lemon juice	15ml/1 tbsp
Chocolate vermicelli (Chocolate sprinkles)	30ml/2 tbsp

Mix the cornflakes with the chopped nuts and divide into four bowls.

Combine the raisins with the banana and apple and place on top of the cornflakes.

Mix the milk with honey and lemon juice and pour over the cornflakes. Sprinkle with chocolate vermicelli and serve.

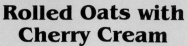

Rolled Oats with Cherry Cream

Ingredients — Metric/Imperial

Ingredients	Metric/Imperial
Rolled oats	200g/7oz
Freshly squeezed orange juice	225ml/8fl oz
Morello cherries, stoned	250g/9oz
Vanilla essence	6 drops/6 drops
Whipping cream	225ml/8fl oz
Cinnamon	a pinch/a pinch
Crème fraîche	225g/8oz
Honey	45ml/3 tbsp

Divide the oats on to four plates and pour the orange juice on top.

Combine the cherries with the vanilla essence and whipped cream. Flavour with cinnamon. Fold in the crème fraîche, sweeten to taste with honey, add to the oats and serve.

Tip

Experiment by replacing the rolled oats with other grain flakes, such as wheat, rye or barley.

Buttermilk Flakes with Honey

Ingredients	Metric/Imperial
Rolled oats	200g/7oz
Buttermilk	½l/18fl oz
Honey	60ml/4 tbsp
Flaked almonds	100g/4oz
Kiwi fruit (Chinese gooseberries)	2/2
Strawberries	100g/4oz
Redcurrants	100g/4oz
Oranges	2/2

Divide the oats on to four plates.

Combine the buttermilk, honey and almonds. Mix with the oats.

Peel and finely dice the kiwi fruit.

Wash and halve the strawberries.

Wash and drain the redcurrants.

Separate the oranges into segments, then cut into small pieces. Mix the fruit, then add to the oats and serve.

Apple Sorbet with Mint

Ingredients — Metric/Imperial

Ingredients	Metric/Imperial
Slightly sour apples	4 large/4 large
White wine	225ml/8fl oz
Water	100ml/4fl oz
Honey	75ml/5 tbsp
Lemon	1/1
Mint	6 leaves/6 leaves

Peel, core and finely dice the apples. Add to the wine and water and purée with a food processor. Add the honey and

lemon juice. Transfer to a freezer-proof dish and freeze.

Occasionally stir the sorbet with a spoon while it is freezing. Just before it sets, stir in the finely chopped mint.

Before serving, whisk the ice with a handmixer and transfer to individual glasses.

Home-Made Almond Ice Cream

Ingredients — Metric/Imperial

Ingredients	Metric/Imperial
Eggs	4/4
Honey	80g/3oz
Vanilla essence	6 drops/6 drops
Whipping cream	100ml/4fl oz
Anisette liqueur	50ml/2 fl oz

Additionally:

Whipped cream	225ml/8fl oz
Butter or margarine	30ml/2 tbsp
Flaked almonds	75ml/6 tbsp

Whisk the eggs with the honey and vanilla essence until creamy. Whisk the cream until very stiff.

Combine the egg mixture, cream and Anisette liqueur. Transfer to a freezer-proof bowl and place in the freezer compartment of the fridge.

For serving, transfer to individual bowls. Decorate with a spoonful of cream.

Heat the butter or margarine in pan and toast the almonds in it. Sprinkle on top of the cream.

Mixed Fruit Salad with Nuts

Ingredients	Metric/Imperial
Strawberries	100g/4oz
Blackberries	100g/4oz
Mango	1/1
Kiwi fruits	2/2
Cantaloupe melon	1 small/1 small
Pistachios, chopped	50g/2oz
Walnuts, chopped	50g/2oz
Pine kernels, chopped	50g/2oz
Maraschino liqueur	6cl/4 tbls
Crème fraîche	225ml/8fl oz
Yoghurt	225ml/8fl oz
Vanilla essence	a few drops/a few drops
Honey	30ml/2 tbsp

Hull the strawberries and blackberries, wash and drain well, then place in a bowl, Peel the mango and dice, then add to the berries. Peel the kiwi fruit and dice. Halve and seed the melon, scoop out the flesh and finely dice. Add with the kiwis and the nuts to the other fruit and combine carefully. Sprinkle the liqueur on top and leave to marinate for 30 minutes.

Combine the crème fraîche with the yoghurt, the vanilla essence and the honey to make a smooth mixture.

Arrange the fruit salad in individual bowls, cover with the cream and serve.

Cook's note: In winter you can make a delicious fruit salad from oranges, apples, grapefruits, pineapple, and bananas.

Semolina Slices with Raspberry Sauce

Ingredients	Metric/Imperial
Milk	1 l/1¾ pt
Salt	a pinch/a pinch
Vanilla essence	6 drops/6 drops
Grated rind of lemon	5 ml/1 tsp
Honey	45–60ml/ 3–4 tbsp
Semolina	250g/9oz
Eggs, beaten	2–3/2–3
Oil for frying	

For the raspberry sauce:

Fresh raspberries	250g/9oz
Crème fraîche	100g/4oz
Honey	30–45ml/ 2–3 tbsp
Cinnamon	a pinch/a pinch
Brandy, gin or kirsch	50ml/2fl oz

Bring the milk and salt to the boil.

Add the vanilla essence and lemon rind. Sweeten to taste with honey.

Pour in the semolina, stirring constantly. Simmer for 10–15 minutes, stirring occasionally, until the mixture thickens.

Remove from the heat, then vigorously stir in the eggs.

Spread on to a wooden board, moistened with water, or into a baking tin, likewise moistened. Cool completely, then cut in slices.

Shallow fry in hot oil.

To make the raspberry sauce, wash and drain the berries well. Purée the raspberries with the crème fraîche. Sweeten with honey and flavour with cinnamon. Aromatize with the brandy or liqueur, then leave to cool in the fridge.

Arrange the semolina slices on serving dishes and spoon the sauce on top.

Tip

The semolina slices taste best when still warm. The raspberry sauce should be warm as well.

You can also sprinkle the slices with a combination of cinnamon and sugar.

Viennese Pudding with Pistachio Nuts and Orange Sauce

Ingredients	Metric/Imperial
Milk	300ml/10fl oz
Salt	a pinch/a pinch
Semolina	50g/2oz
Butter	20g/¾oz
Egg yolks	3/3
Honey	30ml/2 tbsp
Egg whites	3/3
Icing sugar (Confectioner's sugar)	60 ml/4 tbsp

Additionally:

Oil for greasing	
Wholemeal breadcrumbs	60ml/4 tbsp

For the sauce:

Oranges	4/4
Honey	30ml/2 tbsp
Pistachios	30ml/2 tbsp
Raisins	30ml/2 tbsp
White wine	225ml/8fl oz
Orange liqueur	50ml/2fl oz

Bring the milk, salt, semolina and butter to the boil and leave the semolina to fully soak.

Whisk the egg yolks with the honey until fluffy, then fold into the hot semolina. Leave to cool.

Beat the egg whites to form stiff peaks and fold in the icing sugar. Gradually fold into the semolina.

Grease a pudding basin, sprinkle with the bread-crumbs and fill with the semolina. Steam in a double boiler for 30 minutes.

In the meantime, separate the oranges into segments and remove the skins. Add to a pan with the honey, pistachios, raisins and wine. Cook for 5 minutes.

Remove from the heat and

aromatize with the liqueur. Turn the pudding out, spoon the sauce over it and serve.

Pancakes with Almond-Quark

Ingredients Metric/Imperial

Eggs 3/3
Milk 250ml/9fl oz
Mineral water 75ml/5 tbsp
Wholemeal flour 100g/4 oz
Honey 45ml/3 tbsp
Salt a pinch/a pinch
Oil for frying

For the stuffing:

Low-fat quark 125g/4½oz
Crème fraîche 225ml/8fl oz
Grated rind of
lemon 5ml/1tsp
Vanilla essence a few drops/a
few drops
Almond flakes 100g/4oz
Almond liqueur 45ml/3 tbsp

Additionally:

Oil for frying

Combine the eggs with the milk, the mineral water, the flour, the honey and the salt to make a smooth batter. Heat the oil in a frying pan and fry thin pancakes. Remove and keep warm.

Whisk the quark with the crème fraîche, the lemon rind and the vanilla essence. Stir in the almond flakes and the liqueur and spread the quark mixture on the pancakes. Roll up the pancakes, place in layers in a greased shallow dish and bake for 10–15 minutes at 200°C/400°F/Gas 6, remove and serve immediately.

Tutti-Frutti Jelly

Ingredients Metric/Imperial

Strawberries 100g/4oz
Redcurrants 100g/4oz
Raspberries 100g/4oz
Blackberries 100g/4oz
White wine 225ml/8fl oz
Orange juice 450ml/16fl oz
Vanilla essence 6 drops/6 drops
Honey 30ml/2 tbsp
Gelatine,
powder (soaked
in ½ cup water) 25g/1oz
Red food
colouring 4 drops/4 drops
Lemon balm, or
mint 6 leaves/6 leaves
Whipping cream 225ml/8fl oz

Place the berries in a pan with the wine and orange juice. Bring to the boil then add the vanilla essence and honey.

Add the soaked gelatine and food colouring, then transfer the jelly to individual glasses.

Sprinkle with finely chopped lemon balm or mint and leave to set in the fridge.

Spoon the whipped cream on top and serve.

Index